We Happy Few

*"A very fresh account of one man's wartime experience;
this is exactly the kind of history I like the best"*
Louis de Bernières

We Happy Few

Wartime Writings 1939 – 1945

Richard M. Wicker

Edited by
David Bradford

Matador
9 Priory Business Park,
Wistow Road, Kibworth Beauchamp,
Leicestershire. LE8 0RX
Tel: 0116 279 2299
Email: books@troubador.co.uk
Web: www.troubador.co.uk/matador
Twitter: @matadorbooks

ISBN 978 1838590 383

British Library Cataloguing in Publication Data.
A catalogue record for this book is available from the British Library.

Printed and bound by CPI Group (UK) Ltd, Croydon, CR0 4YY
Typeset in 11pt Bembo by Troubador Publishing Ltd, Leicester, UK
Cover illustration: Simon Scarsbrook

Matador is an imprint of Troubador Publishing Ltd

For Wynn

CONTENTS

FOREWORD BY THE
AUTHOR'S DAUGHTER

My father, Richard Wicker, was born on 27th April 1913, and raised in the village of Mayfield, East Sussex. The third youngest of nine siblings, Richard left school aged twelve and for the next nine years worked a series of casual jobs to help support his family, before finding full-time employment as a dairy worker for South Eastern Farmers. He began training as a Royal Air Force volunteer reservist in April 1939, and on 22nd June 1940 was posted to 44 Squadron at RAF Waddington in Lincolnshire to commence active service in the Second World War.

I knew nothing of Dad's wartime writings until summer 2016 when my sister Carole casually mentioned 'Dad's book'. Dad's what? She even quoted to me the first line from memory: "*The snow was falling fast and lay thick around me*" – which apparently Dad had often quoted to her. I was intrigued and taken aback; how had I known nothing about it?

Carole happily gave me her copy: thirty-nine typed A4 pages in a tattered brown envelope. Dad had written the original by hand, and at some point in the late 1940s his sister-in-law Marion, wife of his youngest brother Ray, had typed it up – presumably for posterity or eventual publication. Dad died suddenly from a heart attack in November 1980, aged sixty-seven – the age I am now. Holding in my hands his labour of love, his irreplaceable, unpublished war story, felt almost overwhelming. Strange as this may seem, I couldn't bring myself to read it and tucked it away for safekeeping in my bedroom dresser.

At around the same time, I learned from my brother Martin that he possessed an old, battered travel trunk full of Dad's wartime letters, photos and paraphernalia. When finally I showed this treasure trove, along with the manuscript, to my son David, he was immediately engrossed, fascinated to learn first-hand about the grandfather he never knew. Throwing himself into transcribing and editing, David set to work creating the published book you hold in your hands today.

Meanwhile, I was moved to learn from Dad's letters of his deep love for his parents and siblings, and his conviction not to marry until he was absolutely certain he had found the right woman. As it happened, he found her just down the road, in his home village of Mayfield. His beloved wife, our dear mum, is now ninety and still remembers their first meeting. Dad's letters reveal that their courtship got off to a stormy, faltering start: he preferred the quiet and solitude of the countryside, while she liked to socialise and go to dances.

Recalling Dad's daily writing ritual, Mum is certain that he hoped to have this manuscript published. Unable or unwilling to speak to us about the war, in writing he found a way to unburden himself of the trauma he had been through while giving free rein to his indisputable talent. In doing so, he has revealed to us his hidden depths and allowed us to see a man more complex and more tormented by the past than the doting, playful father we had known and so dearly loved.

Mum now lives in a care home, and failing sight has sadly curtailed her love of reading, but when I read aloud to her Dad's book — finally an actual book! — tears rolled down our cheeks as together we relived his long-awaited return from war — *the green fields of England, I have seen them again* — and his private prayer to *the many boys who have died for me*. Dad was among the happy few who made it home; this book is his tribute to all those who did not.

Janet Bradford, February 2019

ONE

Northern Germany, Winter 1940

The snow was falling fast and lay thick around me. I pushed the lapel of my coat up under my throat again with numbed fingers, and as I glanced across the square to the statue of Wilhelm der Grosse a heavily laden sleigh pulled by two very lean horses lumbered towards me.

Making sure there was no traffic approaching the crossroads, either from the narrow road from the seafront or from Gartenstrasse, which led out past the gasworks and the harbour, I signalled to the driver to go on. Sitting up on the front of the sleigh, white like a figure made from icing sugar, he raised his whip as he passed. I lifted a hand in salute, then fell to studying the tracks of the sleigh as it disappeared round the corner by the *Bäckerei*.

As I put my hand back into my coat pocket, my fingers encountered a two-and-a-half-inch nail and I thought to myself, *I must put that somewhere safe before I go in at the gate.*

It made me hungry again, the thought of going back in. These were my only breaks from hunger: moments when my brain was too preoccupied to receive my stomach's urgent, persistent messages clamouring for food.

Suddenly, the rattling of a tractor broke the almost eerie silence. As it drew into the square, its industrious panting exploded into deafening reverberations. Drawn behind it caterpillar-like were three large trailers laden with potatoes. I forgot my hunger again as I concentrated on the cargo.

As silence fell again, I turned the potatoes over in my hands: two in each coat pocket, two each for Wainwright and me for supper tonight. My thoughts turned to how grateful I was for Wainwright's companionship. Unlike many of the others who were from middle- and high-class homes, he was scrupulously clean and tidy. His bed space, blankets and utensils were always kept exceedingly neat and clean, and he had that air about him, the air of a man who savours cleanness even while he's trapped in a life of filth and degradation. We were living among humans deprived of all amenities and who behaved almost as animals.

I must have presented a ludicrous figure to passers-by, standing there, shabbily dressed, in the middle of the square in that little Baltic fishing village. On my feet, German jackboots with uncomfortable wooden soles; overtop my Air Force tunic and held about my middle with a piece of rope, a sky-blue Polish overcoat many sizes too large for me; and on my head, a brown beret. Having gone two months without shaving, my beard had grown a full six-and-a-half inches below my chin – a beard to be proud of.

People certainly stared at me. Tiny, spindly-legged children escorting still tinier children home from school or on shopping expeditions. Old men. Women of all ages, too, some of them young and attractive, who little thought as they passed that beneath this old-man exterior there stood a young man with a young man's desires, thoughts, hopes and vitality. A romantic, a lover of solitude and the little things in life: a stroll down a leafy lane with a girlfriend, the beauty of flowers, a sunset, the noise of the waves on the seashore, the wind and the rain lashing my face, a walk on the Downs, the glorious warmth of the sun, the romance of moonlight, the mystery of the stars, the fresh greenness of the countryside in spring, the fragrant scent of hay and honeysuckle in the summer, the breathtaking loveliness of autumn foliage in October, and the cosy satisfaction of a book, a pipe and a log fire on winter evenings. All these things were a part of me. I clamoured for no big cities, bright lights, expensive parties, exclusive restaurants and gay dance halls. Just a simple fellow, loving the simple little things in life: the things from which my soul derived its entire existence and from which I had been so suddenly and ruthlessly uprooted and flung out upon a sea of chaos.

I was fortunate in having been born a very adaptable character. I seldom revolted against the environment I found myself enduring. When I had a long, arduous and seemingly impossible task ahead of me, I would plod on and on and see it through. If I was caught out in a drenching thundershower, I would not take shelter until I'd reached my journey's end. As a child, if I had to hold a log or piece of iron in position for my father, I would hold it there until it was fixed, though every muscle in my body might be crying out to be relaxed.

Yet there were to be times when my spirit and my body would break down under stress of things unbearable. Times when I would lose faith in God and all humanity. Times when, so depraved by hunger, heartbreak, anguish of soul and torment of mind, by the indescribable longing and yearning over long years of physical and spiritual degradation in captivity, I would think I had endured all that it was possible to endure. In these moments, I would cry out to the God in whom I had lost faith to let me die: "End this, my miserable existence, oh God. I can stand no more. Let me die tonight, let me just fall asleep and not awaken unto the morning. Let them find me dead on the straw that I may find relief in death. Let those who love me weep for me and those who hate me forgive me for whatever I've done to create that hatred. Bless my father and mother and sisters and brothers. Let my death relieve them of that awful anxiety for my safety which they must constantly endure."

But such times were still ahead of me. We were still saying it cannot last more than a year. Lovely memories of pre-war joys still lived in our hearts. We could still close our eyes and float back to the green fields of England in springtime, still see the tearful smiles of our loved ones as we last said goodbye. We could still feel the warmth of wife, mother or sweetheart. I could still remember every detail of my last evening in Mayfield.

TWO

We had a very lovely walk in the afternoon, not a very long one but long enough that a beautiful variety of scenes, flowers, scents, birds and all that belonged to the countryside had been presented to us. It was 3rd August 1940. What a job I'd had getting my leave to coincide with her holiday. Letters, telegrams, interviews with flight commander, more telegrams.

> *Regret, cannot make it. Please see your matron for 27-3rd.*
> *Matron insists I stick to previous arrangements. Letter following.*

My darling Ricky,
Oh, you must do something at your end to make it all right for us to be together for our holiday. I cannot bear the thought of holiday unless I can spend, well, almost all of it with you.

I went to the matron, like you asked me, but she didn't seem to think it all that important that you and I should be together this holiday. 'There are other nurses to take holiday, you know, Lodge,' she said, 'and they have equally good reasons for wishing to keep to their present arrangements. Even if your young man is in the Air Force, no doubt many of the other nurses have boyfriends or husbands in the services, and they could all come crying to me to let them have holidays, this week or that, to spend with people.'

And then she suddenly became more kindly and got up from behind her desk and came round to me and put her hand on my shoulder. 'You're a nurse now, Lodge,' she said, 'and whatever instinct prompted you to join this very noble profession, you knew you would be called upon to make certain sacrifices, that other people's needs must come before your own, that you had to be prepared to give up in service all selfish desires of your own heart. We are very short of trained nurses, as you know, and while the holidays are on, those of us who are left to carry on will have to be on our feet 15 to 18 hours a day. We have got another batch of injured coming in from last night's raid today, and I don't know where we're going to put them or who will attend to them. I dare say it means a very great deal to you to spend your holiday with this young man of yours; it also means a very great deal to the sick and injured in this hospital that they are nursed back to health and strength as quickly as possible — just as it means a very great deal to our country that we get these injured airmen and soldiers and sailors back to duty. Your young man will wait. It will not be long anyway, and I'm sure he'll arrange something and you'll both have a very lovely time together. Now, run along and think about that, and if you still want to go in the morning, come and see me again.'

That night, I was put on casualty ward. I think Matron must have arranged it purposely. Oh, it was dreadful, Ricky. Seven of them were airmen from plane crashes. One had his face almost entirely burnt away; just his eyes looked through a slit in the bandaging and they seemed to follow me about the ward like the eyes of an injured dog, begging me to do something for him. Another one was in the same plane; it crash-landed or something and caught fire. He is burnt almost all over but not his face. We don't think he will live. He keeps talking all the time, delirious. 'Rosemary,' he says, 'you must know I didn't mean that, Rosemary. Give me the letter back. I know Geoff is only a friend; I was crazy with jealousy and I want you back, Rosemary' — and so on, all night. He'll not live another night out. He'll never see his Rosemary again, Ricky.

Oh, my darling, I can't leave until my proper time. I can't come and leave all this agony and misery for others to attend to. Try again, my darling, to postpone your leave, we'll have such a lovely time down in dear old Sussex. You can show me all your little walks and we can lie under the trees and you can talk to me. I love listening to you talking to me, Ricky. Everything you say seems so sincere and straight from your heart.

And there is something I so very dreadfully want to hear you say. Why won't you say it, Ricky? I do love you so much, and yet you are only, well, so very nice to me, without ever saying what I want you to. Now, enough of this. Put this letter on the fire, or wherever you put all your poor little love letters, and go and make love to your CO at once and tell him it means so much to us to be together for a little while. He'll understand.

All my love, darling.

Ever yours,

Connie.

I carried that letter to Kiel and back that night.[1] It wasn't a dreadfully exciting trip but like most crews in those days, we were very lacking in experience and equipment. At a quarter past three the next morning, our ETA for the English coast had expired by twenty-five minutes and the navigator was getting worried. We were still over the sea, hovering over it as though stationary. All around was pitch darkness, not a star, not a friendly light anywhere. Only a pitch-black night with the slightly less black sea beneath us scattered with moving white wave tips.

I had been pounding on the Morse key for the last half an hour, appealing desperately to Heaton, Heston, Hall and Newcastle for a fix. I'd had no answering call from them. From the chaotic melee of signals and atmospherics, I detected almost every conceivable combination of cipher, except that which constituted my own call sign: CR8.J.

I was just a sprog. At the outbreak of war, this country of ours was caught, as they say, with its trousers down. I was among the first of the RAFVR wireless operators

---

1   Kiel is the capital and most populous city in the northern German state of Schleswig-Holstein.

to go into operation in June 1940.[2] We were without all those navigational aids which later would eliminate almost entirely the dangers of navigational failure that could result in an aircraft being lost. We arrived on the target by dead reckoning and with the aid of homing on German beacons. We found our objective by going down low enough to see it with our eyes, and we got back by the grace of God.

Many ran out of petrol before they reached Britain's coast; the North Sea closed over them. Many, through faulty instruments affected by the varied atmospheric conditions throughout their 1,000 to 1,500-mile night-long trip flew straight out into the Atlantic and perished. Many more fell victim to German flak or night-fighters; some to engine failure and some to interception of their wireless messages.

Desperately I had to cast around in my mind to recall some advice that had been given to us by our radio instructor: tune back on your station, harmonise transmitter to receiver, maximum aerial current, check accumulators, change to HF coils. Oh, what's the use? Nothing is of any use anymore. You're a failure, you've let your crew down. You'll run out of petrol and drop into the cold black North Sea. You won't see her anymore. You won't see your mother and father and sisters and brothers anymore. Goodbye beloved walks through my woods and fields, goodbye to the intoxicating scent of honeysuckle and new-mown hay.

---

2   The RAF Volunteer Reserve was formed in July 1936 to provide individuals to supplement the Royal Auxiliary Air Force. By the end of 1941 more than half of Bomber Command aircrew were members of the RAFVR.

'To every man upon this Earth, death cometh soon or late.'[3]
'If you can force your heart and nerve and sinew / To serve your turn.'[4]

I was more used to working HF coils. Very, very faintly I heard my call sign. Right in the back of a crowded hall, as it were, a friend was trying to make himself heard to me, while all around me people chanted and screamed deafening, raucous noises into my ear to distract me and to overcome that still small voice of calm. There it was again, I'd not imagined it. CR8.J. CR8.J. CR8.J. We got home at a quarter past six, operation as detailed. Bombs were seen to explode on the deck of the Scharnhorst.[5]

I presented myself to the flight commander at a quarter past two.

"You mustn't forget there is a war on, Sergeant. We are not at all well off for radio operators yet, you know. Can't hold up the whole crew and lay a machine idle just because you want to go off and make love to a girlfriend for fourteen days."

"Um, only seven days, sir."

"I'm sorry, Sergeant?"

"It's my air crew's regulation leave, sir."

"It is only a regulation provided others are available to fill the spaces."

"I've been up here nearly two months, sir."

---

3   From 'Horatius', the first poem in the collection *Lays of Ancient Rome*, by Thomas Babington Macaulay, first published in 1842.

4   From the poem 'If—' by Rudyard Kipling, first published in 1910.

5   Scharnhorst was a German capital ship of Nazi Germany's Kriegsmarine, finally sunk during the Battle of the North Cape on 26th December 1943, by the Royal Navy battleship HMS Duke of York.

"How many operations?"

"Eleven, sir."

"You don't qualify until two months are up. You must wait until your crew go on leave. You are not yet overdue, Sergeant, though you may be due for seven days' leave. Come to me again in a week's time. That will be all, Sergeant."

"Very good, sir."

Sir,

I, 746715 etc, etc, respectfully request etc, etc, in view of my having lost regulation leave by changes to three different crews and aircraft etc, etc.

I append my girlfriend's latest telegram, etc, etc. From July 22 to August 3.

I am, sir, etc, etc.

At four o'clock a runner found me in the hangar. Across my application, the commanding officer had blue-pencilled: 'Granted. In future, you shall apply through the usual channels.'

At five o'clock the next morning, I was waiting for the barber at Euston Station to start work. I had been travelling all night and badly needed a shave before taking the first train out of Victoria on my last stage south into Sussex.

THREE

It was just getting dark. 3rd August 1940 was drawing to a close. I felt her shiver slightly and I held her a little closer to me as we walked up over the steep towards the vicarage woods.

"Cold?"

"Oh, no, no, Ricky, I'm not cold."

"You shivered."

"Well, this is our last night, Ricky."

"Yes. Still, it's been a wonderful week."

"Oh yes, I've loved every minute of it, Ricky. Do you realise, we might not see each other anymore? I'm so dreadfully afraid that one night you might not come back. You can't believe the agony I suffer hearing them say, 'One of our aircraft failed to return'."

"I shall always come back, Connie."

"You don't know."

"I do."

"You're just trying to stop me worrying."

We had reached the row of trees on the knoll. I spread my coat beneath one of them, sat down and then reached up, caught her hands and pulled her down to me. I kissed her and held her to me tightly and, with her cheek against mine, looked over her shoulder, down into the woods we'd just left.

She was right, I thought, we would never see each other again. One by one my pals had disappeared. Missing, presumed dead, killed in action: aircraft last seen descending in flames. So many ways of dying in bombing raids. We sat there quietly holding each other closely. The edge of the moon peeped over the tops of the trees. Yes, you are right, Connie. We shall never see each other again.

I lived that night over again, the night I had experienced a week before coming on leave, the night of 17th July. The target was Paderborn Aircraft Park,[6] and we had done two runs over it at 12,000ft, dropping 250s and incendiaries. Every conceivable type of defence was being used against us. Flak burst all around, above and below us; cannon tracer shells flashed past like rockets. Flaming onions hung in the sky a little below us.[7]

Both pilot and navigator were happy-go-lucky, devil-may-care types, both Canadians from Montreal, both pilot officers.

---

6   Paderborn is a city in eastern North Rhine-Westphalia, Germany, capital of the Paderborn district.

7   The flaming onion was a type of anti-aircraft fire that used a visible tracer, the name referring to both the gun, and especially the flares it fired. All five rounds were discharged as rapidly as possible, giving the 'string of flaming onions' effect.

"You'd better get down a bit now, Walker, and we'll have a look, see the damage," navigator Romans said to the pilot over the intercom.

"Well, I don't know, you know. They're getting a bit close with this bloody stuff, don't you think?"

"Oh, that's alright, man, they'll never hit us."

"They'll never hit us? Huh! Famous last words."

"Oh, you and your famous last words. Let's go down, Walker."

"OK, down we go."

Those were indeed to be his very last words. The tail of the old Hampden rose as I sat and watched the hand of my altimeter fall back faster and faster as we gathered speed in a crazy dive towards the now blazing aerodrome.[8] Vibration and the gush of wind past us rose to a crescendo. Great white fingers of light swept the sky in search of us. Balls of fire exploded in my face. All around the sky was a picture of kaleidoscopic, terrifying beauty. I made sure my ammunition pans were properly fixed on my two VGOs,[9] set them at fire and sat back and waited for those brief seconds of opportunity to fire on the enemy as we swept over the aerodrome.

---

8   The Handley Page Hampden was an RAF twin-engine medium bomber, often referred to by aircrews as the 'Flying Suitcase' because of its cramped crew conditions. From *Handley Page Hampden*, published by World Heritage Encyclopedia: 'Almost half of the Hampdens built, 714, were lost on operations, taking with them 1,077 crew killed and another 739 missing. German flak accounted for 108, one hit a German barrage balloon, 263 Hampdens crashed because of 'a variety of causes' and 214 others were classed as 'missing'. Luftwaffe pilots claimed 128 Hampdens, shooting down 92 at night... [It was] withdrawn from Bomber Command in 1942.'

9   Vickers Gas Operated (VGO) machine guns.

Five-thousand feet. He surely wouldn't go much lower. Four-thousand feet... 3,000... 2,000... 1,500... Base of dive over target. Suddenly I saw hangars and flames and aircraft in crazy shapes and little tiny figures running in all directions, and almost at the same instant there was an intense blinding flash. I felt the Hampden give a sickening, stumbling lurch. We had levelled off, and now the tail fell and we were climbing steeply.

I suddenly realised we were in extreme quiet: no vibration, no engine noise. I began to panic. Feathered engines at this angle? I hoped those damned fools knew what they were doing. And then, in the middle of this crazy nightmare, my headphone crackled and I heard a human voice.

"Hello pilot, navigator here. Hello pilot, navigator here. What's happened to our power? Hey, Walker, you alright? Hey, Walker?"

The navigator's voice has risen with each sentence. The last 'Hey, Walker' was almost shouted. We were almost vertical now, still climbing under the impetus of our dive but losing speed fast. Slower, slower and ever slower. We must have been approaching stalling speed, the tail coming up, about to nosedive straight into the deck. I made up my mind, reached out and tugged at the jettison cord of my escape hatch. I pushed, hammered and kicked frantically: the escape hatch wouldn't drop.

Oh, darling, you must do something at your end to make it all right for us to be together for our holiday. I love listening to you talking, Ricky, so sincere and straight from your heart.

Why don't you say it, Ricky? Tell them it means so much to us to be together for a little while.

All my love, my darling.

And then I heard engine noise again, felt us level off and accelerate. I switched on my microphone:

"Hello pilot, hello pilot. Rear gunner to pilot."

No reply.

"Hello navigator. Hello navigator… Hello navigator. Rear gunner to navigator."

No reply. Intercom shot away, probably. I knew I'd better go up and fix it. Then the wings waggled.

I crawled up to the pilot's cabin. He was sagging back, unconscious with terrible head injuries. The port side of his cabin was entirely shot away. Romans was leaning across him controlling the aircraft. He had achieved the impossible. In those few brief seconds from his 'Hey Walker' shout to the time I was about to abandon aircraft, he had crawled back along his tunnel, its walls cluttered with equipment, scrambled up through a 12-inch slit in the Astra hatch and made his way along to the pilot. He had flung Walker's hands from the closed throttle controls, opened the throttle and pushed forward the control column.

It took us half an hour to extricate Walker and drag him back along the Astra hatch, by which point my Sidcot suit was smothered in blood. We bandaged his head, got Romans settled at the controls, and I perused maps as we staggered on through the night. Eventually we found base and had to wait for four other aircraft to land before us.

I nursed Walker's head in my lap to soften the jar as we touched down.

We swung round and raced across the field to the hangars and awaiting ambulances, doctors and nurses for whom we had radioed ahead. As we approached them, Romans realised he had no brakes – our hydraulics had been shot away. Reacting intuitively, he tipped up onto one wing to stop us running into the ambulances and awaiting medics. There was no stopping the momentum as we bumped over the commanding officer's car, the adjutant's car and the gun pit, tearing the bottom out of the aircraft before we finally came to rest.

Walker died as the ambulance drove out of the gate on the way to the hospital.

FOUR

"Why are you crying, Connie?"

"I don't know whether it's because I am very happy or very sad."

"Oh, come on now, this won't do. You're a very lovely, healthy girl. You're on holiday, you're young. You've a good, noble profession, lots of friends, nice teeth, nice hair, lovely eyes, a captivating smile, pretty legs, gentle hands, kissable lips. It's a very lovely evening: quiet, peaceful, the air is cool and scented with honeysuckle. I'm here and you're here. There is nobody near to see or hear us."

"Don't, Ricky," she broke in. "You're not in love with me, are you? I'm such a nice girl, such a grand little pal. You're so awfully fond of me, but…"

"Is that why you're crying, Connie? Look, my darling, let's not get all serious tonight. Love is far too serious a thing for us to discuss on our last evening together. Let's talk about what we are going to do on my next leave, or when the war's over, or about religion or the stars. Can you recognise the Orion constellation? Straight through there, look. He's the Greek hunter. That one, out on its own, is his little dog running ahead of him. There's one of his legs, there's the other. There's one of his upraised arms. See, Betelgeuse. See the belt around the waist?"

She said nothing, so I went on:

"You know, your eyes are rather lovely after you've been crying. In fact, you're rather lovely altogether tonight. I think moonlight becomes you."

Still she did not respond.

"Look, my darling, you asked, do I love you? I don't know. And if I did, this wouldn't be the right time to tell you. This time tomorrow, we might be 1,000 miles apart. Let's take life and accept it as it is at the moment. The future is so uncertain. We can't plan ahead. These are our last few moments. Let's enjoy them, take every ounce of pleasure they hold."

I pressed her shoulders back onto the turf behind her. The ground beneath us trembled and then came the *wump, wump, wump* of bombs falling in the distance. Instinctively she clutched me more closely to her and my blood raced. I fumbled recklessly with her dress.

"No, Ricky, we…"

I laid my lips on hers and kissed her into silence. It was to be my first experience, and I was tremendously excited as my exploring hands encountered silken undies and smooth, warm flesh. I began to wish she would help me – I didn't seem to be able to negotiate the intricacies of her underwear as easily as I'd hoped. She was trembling and breathing heavily. I withdrew my hand, placed it under her shoulders, and with both arms around her drew her up to me and kissed her trembling lips passionately. For a long moment I held her, then we fell slightly apart and looked into each other's eyes.

"Don't you want me, Connie?" I asked, very softly.

She dropped her eyes and cuddled close up to me again but said nothing.

"Connie?"

"Yes, I do, Ricky, more than you know, but, well, I just think we oughtn't to, not before… Well, after all, there is plenty of time for that after one is married. Besides, something might happen."

"No it won't, Connie. This constant repression of one's desires is more harmful than the possible consequences. Connie, if you loved me, you would be happy to do anything for me. You would give up anything for me; you would give yourself up happily and willingly—"

"To someone who doesn't love me?" she broke in. "Oh no, Ricky, I'm not such a fool. I do love you. I love you so dreadfully that it's painful to be away from you, even for a little while, yet you treat me so lightly. You say, 'Oh, Connie won't mind about this and that.' You don't realise how much I do mind. You talk blithely of letters from Ruby or Amy or Nora or Olive and your other various girlfriends, little realising the stab in the heart it gives me. You don't know anything about love, Ricky. You call it wishy-washy sentiment and expect me to flirt light-heartedly with you and be good pals and things like that. It goes deeper than that with me. I want you, yes, but I want you spiritually as well as physically. You want to possess my body; I want to possess your heart – to know that you love me, that you care for me as much as I do for you – then you can take me and do what you like with me."

She looked very lovely sitting there facing me with both hands on the lapels of my tunic, the moonlight playing on her hair.

"I see," I said.

"You're not angry with me, Ricky?"

"No, no, my darling, I'm not angry with you. You're so lovely and desirable tonight. I could so easily say that I loved you tonight and claim you tonight, but it wouldn't be quite true."

"There's somebody else, Ricky?" she asked.

"No, no one in particular, darling, but I just can't seem to be able to honestly say that I love you and only you with all my heart and soul and strength. I wish I could. I wish I could take my heart out of my breast and hold it out to you in my cupped hands so that you could literally take possession of it and cherish it. It's such an unresponsive thing, Connie. You spoke of others. Yes, there have been and are lots of others; some of them felt and feel the same as you do. My heart doesn't warm to any of them. I love them all a little bit, but not one with all my heart."

"And I suppose they all—" she broke off, confused.

"Oh no, my darling, not any of them. I don't think of them that way. I've always tried to play the game. I try not to take any more out of life than I can put back, and I know I can't put very much into their lives."

"Why did you particularly want me tonight, Ricky?"

"Because you're closer to my heart tonight. Because, well, I suppose because—"

"Because you mightn't have another chance."

"Well, yes. You might say because I may not have another chance."

"Would it be very wrong, Ricky?"

"Would what? You mean—"

She had fallen back onto the turf, her hands folded beneath the nape of her neck. I looked down at her and she smiled up at me tremulously. I had never fought so hard within myself. I pressed down to her and she held herself against me, vibrant and passionate.

"You really do love me, Connie, don't you?"

"I'm willing to prove it, if you want me still."

"No, I can't let you, Connie."

"Please, Ricky."

"No, my darling, it's awfully late." I looked at my watch. "Gosh, it's a-quarter-to-one. Do you realise, we're catching the nine o'clock train?"

I leapt up, caught her by the hands and pulled her to me again. She clung to me, her face wet with tears. We stood there a long time beneath that tree in the moonlight, then we walked slowly and without speaking up the rest of the sloping field to the roadway and the Singer sportscar I was using.

It would be over five years before either of us saw that tree again: she would stand and cry in my arms again, this time because our romance was completely over.

FIVE

So many men with a far greater command of words than I have failed to completely convey to the reader the exhilaration of flying that it would be presumptuous of me to attempt it. The desire to fly was born in me at a very early age. I used to watch those pioneers of flight stagger across the sky at 85 to 100mph with an intense feeling of awe and wonderment. And if I had been old enough then to claim a god to worship, it would surely have been those men who recklessly took their life in their hands and ventured to defy the power of gravity. Men who relied solely on a structure of wood and fabric and an unfaltering internal combustion engine to take them on a journey through space and set them down unharmed at the other end.

Not in their wildest flights of imagination could the Wright brothers have conceived what was to have been the ultimate outcome of their first take-off from terra firma in 1903. In these days of 120-ton aircraft, 2,000hp units, 50,000ft ceilings and speeds of up to 600mph, we're inclined to look on their efforts as puny and amateurish. Half a century of experiment has passed. For many in those early days came hardship and heartbreak, if not death or horrible mutilation as time and again imperfect design resulted in a sudden, sickening crash back to earth.

Yet our scientists, engineers and designers learnt by the death of every pioneer. Today, after the rapid strides made under pressure of necessity in two world wars, an aircraft crashing back to earth makes headline news. The progress of 100 tons of wood and metal non-stop for thousands of miles arouses scarcely more comment than that a child has ridden to school on a bicycle. I, in my turn, never dreamed that I should have an opportunity one day to share in the glory of the aviators.

As a child, I was sick and weakly, small in stature, skinny and bony. I knew I'd never be able to endure the hardships of flight, that my frail frame would never acquire the energy of my feeble brain, nor my brain the intelligence to join the ranks of those chosen few. My parents were poor; while I was still young, my father had to give up what had been years earlier a very prosperous profession. As the horse was slowly but relentlessly replaced as a means of transport by the car and tractor, my blacksmith father fought a hard and bitter fight to obtain a livelihood by other means.

I had seen his yard full of great steaming, stamping carthorses waiting to be re-shod with the heavy shoes that he and his men made at the forge. I had stood and watched fascinated as the great beasts bucked and reared, and even today I can still smell the all-pervading odour of burning hoof as the red-hot shoe was applied. With the car and lorry and tractor came rubber tyres to displace the broad iron wheels my father made for years for the farm carts and Sussex wagons. Gates too, once ironwork, were now factory-made. Hand-forged ploughshares and iron agricultural machinery became things of the past.

Metal now arrived painted in bright blues and reds at the railway station straight from the factory where it was produced much more quickly and cheaply than my father could ever hope to at the forge. At home, my mother produced children with monotonous regularity. My father's income went down and down, his liabilities up and up. Finally he and his partner were obliged to sell up, and what had been the very centre of activity in the village, a veritable hive of industry, was taken over by a placid hot-water plumbing engineer. All that remained were the anvil and the iron rings in the walls – to which great Sussex horses had been tied as they plunged and reared – reminders of those pre-Industrial-Revolution days of prosperity for farriers.

I was my mother's ninth child but only the seventh living one, and when Nurse Carpenter slapped me into life on 27th April 1913, it was doubtful I would survive. The first few years of life would have been no pleasure at all to me, supposing I was able to recall or account for them. I am told that I was constantly sick and ill, and when I started elementary school I'd scarcely ever left my mother's knee. I was broken-hearted to be parted from her loving care for those long periods of the day. As soon as I left for school with my brothers and sisters, I began crying, and continued all the way. Once at school, I snivelled near-continuously, and if I didn't happen to be crying, I was constantly reduced to tears by the taunt of 'old cry-baby', the shameful name I quickly earned for myself from the other boys. It didn't help that my good mother had chosen to crown my Norfolk jacket with a great lace collar which spread generously over my back and shoulders and gave me a very effeminate appearance – quickly seized upon by my enemies who would point at me and cry, 'Cry-baby looks like a girl!'.

Thus my schooldays became an ordeal which I shirked at every opportunity. I was, as I have said, constantly sick, suffering headaches and chilblains, and always seizing on these opportunities to be absent from school. My brothers and sisters soon lost patience with me and were loath to admit to their school friends the fact that this snivelling little brat was their brother. Indeed, I earned yet more obnoxious names from them on account of my excuses for absence from school: I became 'The Little Pretender'.

Nonetheless, amazingly enough, I managed to keep up with my class in most subjects. I was every bit the thinker, and I suppose I employed those long hours lying with headaches and sickness on the sofa of our sitting room very gainfully turning over school problems in my mind. I memorised the poetry I loved, much of which I can still quote fairly accurately today, despite never having read it since. Long extracts from Shakespeare's *Julius*

Caesar or Hubert and Arthur,[10] Henry V at Agincourt,[11] and so on.

The psychological lift of finishing school for the day at 3:45pm caused me to brighten up considerably, and I proved quite a bright, useful lad in the summer evenings. Our straitened circumstances made it necessary for all of us children to have an after-school job – and a before-school job, come to that. I distinctly remember lying in bed awake from 7:15am onwards listening intently for the whistle of the 7:25am train as it rounded Argos Hill curve at the white bridge. This was the train that brought the morning papers to our village. For many years, my sisters and I took turns meeting this train and rushing three or four papers to the residents of a well-to-do corn merchant who did not care to wait for the normal delivery. This earned us tuppence a day or 1 shilling a week, which in those days was a tremendous boost to our family income.

We earned income in multitudinous ways: gathering fallen leaves for the compost heaps of the gentry, picking up balls for the players at the local lawn tennis club, weeding garden paths at a penny an hour, gathering acorns, sweeping away snow, picking bunches of flowers to sell, picking blackberries, and so on. Of course, every halfpenny earned by these means had to be taken home and given to Mother to help buy our shoes and clothes or to be put by to help her give us that very lovely Christmas, which she, despite hardships, always provided.

---

10 From Shakespeare's *King John*.
11 The St Crispin's Day speech from Shakespeare's *Henry V*, Act IV Scene 3.

I venture to say that we were all scrupulously honest regarding the carrying home of these treasured coppers. Indeed, we were tremendously proud to hand them over to Mother, and would compete most eagerly with each other for a job of work when Mrs so-and-so sent round to see if one of the children could do such and such for her. Thus our environment trained us to be honest and hard-working, and my father's status in the village was no whit the less for having failed in business.

He paid his debts at nineteen and six in the pound and remained self-employed,[12] repairing and supplying stoves and kitchen ranges, undertaking repair work to agricultural machinery, ironwork, tin-smithing and chimney cleaning. A job at which he was surely unrivalled was the felling of trees in difficult spaces among buildings and gardens. I'm not exaggerating when I say he could bring down a 50-60ft tree to fall exactly upon a line drawn on the ground at any angle from the base of the trunk. He was still doing this, with the aid of my younger brother and me, at the age of sixty-nine.

I said that our environment trained us nine children to be honest and hard-working. I am very proud to be able to say that, because I can think of no other combination of virtues likely to build up a Christian character in a man or woman. That training, however secular, did us more good than all the years we attended the Baptist Chapel Sunday School – the only evidence for which is the bookshelf at home laden with *Little Gleaner* magazines.

---

12 'Nineteen and six in the pound' was 19 shillings and sixpence, or sixpence short of a pound.

My father was a strict Baptist, but I hope I will never be called upon to explain exactly what that term implies. I never saw him attend a place of worship except for a wedding or funeral – and even then reluctantly. Goodness knows, it's since been job enough to persuade him to attend even the weddings of his own sons and daughters. All his life he has been possessed of a great disinclination to put on his best clothes. It can be said without fear of contradiction that he is not a man who knows how to dress well. He no doubt contrived during his brief courting days to make himself look presentable, but I am prepared to wager a considerable sum of money on the fact that my mother, then a very shy and beautiful young girl blossoming into womanhood, did not choose my father for her husband on account of his being the smartest dressed beau in the village.

As we children grew older and learned the art of clothing, Father and his clothes became a family joke. We'd watch him trying to make himself presentable for the ritual of Sunday afternoon tea. It seemed his neck was somehow incompatible with a collar and tie. After an hour's painful struggling with studs and collars in his bedroom, he would come down dishevelled as ever – to my younger brother's unconcealed, uncontrolled and highly infectious mirth. Perhaps it was our laughter that discouraged Father from making the attempt very often.

Nonetheless, collar and tie or no collar and tie, Father was a strict Baptist and he had inherited at least one law that he observed very strictly unto himself and his children until we outgrew his control: namely, that on the seventh day, thou shalt rest and do no manner of work. To this he added his own sub-law, inflicting on his children a decree that stated very firmly thou shalt not even play on the seventh day. Thus, on the Sabbath, he would allow us no hoops, no skipping rope, no bat, no ball, no hopscotch, no paperchase, no bicycle. Strict Baptist chapel Sunday school 9:30; strict Baptist chapel service 11:15; congregational Sunday school 2:30; tea at 5:00; and bed at 7:00.

As you might have deduced already, Sunday was no glee day for us. Even so, I do not wish to censure my father on this account or portray him as a tyrant feared by his children or hated for his strictness. On the contrary, he was beloved of us all, and whatever views one may have regarding observance of the Sabbath, I feel that he was only doing what was in his own mind the best thing for us.

Since World War Two, great controversy has been aroused by cinemas across the country applying for licences to open to the public on a Sunday. The church is strongly and openly opposed to such action in principle, though it seems unable to offer alternative attractions to prevent young folk from finding mischief for their idle hands to do. If the church, as a dutiful mother, finds it necessary to snatch the knife from the hand of a playful child, she must substitute it for a doll or rattle or some other amusement to keep the child occupied. It is not only the children, either; the fathers and mothers of the next generation won't be content to walk around aimlessly nor to while away the hours sitting in their homes.

The solution to my mind is perfectly obvious: with millions and millions of good books on the shelves of the country's libraries, it should not be difficult to select and adapt to the screen, for special use on a Sunday, some with an intensely strong moral and educational story. These films are already in existence; very few have come from America. However, I digress.

SIX

I don't remember exactly when in my life my health began to improve. I know that nobody would ever believe me when I told them I'd just left school. I was not apprenticed to a trade, I just did odd jobs: a day in the garden for Mrs so-and-so, two days a week for somebody else, a day delivering bread with old Charlie, a day at the radio and cycle shop, and so on. I always gave satisfaction: I was methodical and thorough and energetic. The local gentry loved me to trim their hedges, mow their lawns, dig their gardens and weed their herbaceous borders. Later I graduated to the washing of cars, the building of rock gardens and the pruning of treasured rose trees and fruit trees.

Cars fascinated me. I did a lot of work for a lady and gentleman of Scotch descent. The woman resided here all year round and had a car of her own, and the man, who was connected with tea plantations in India, came home for three months of the year and bought a new car each time. He'd drive it for three months, then sell it just before he went back. Thus I acquired some knowledge of the care and attention needed to ensure good, safe motoring.

In fact, by this time, I had quite a lot of experience on a very wide range of subjects. I look back upon these early years with a very strange mixture of pleasure and regret. Pleasure because I feel that during those years I learnt to square up to any job presented to me, and never to say, 'No, I've never done that before, I don't know how'. There is after all quite a lot to be said for the man who will have a go. It may be true that a little knowledge is a dangerous thing, but supposing one exercises a fair modicum of caution and common sense, a little knowledge can be converted into a very great deal of knowledge. But for the scientists' total disregard for the little-knowledge-being-dangerous theory, we should have no radio, telephones, electricity or means of transport. Likewise, our hospitals would still be overflowing with patients suffering from diseases presumed incurable. Pleasure, then, but also regret.

Regret because even at a time when I still had, I hoped, a large portion of my life ahead of me − unless I met an untimely end − I felt myself a jack of all trades and master of none. Had I been able to devote my life to a specialised job, I felt that I would by now have been a very great success instead of an insignificant nondescript. But we are not all born to be great. I had to be content to play my insignificant part in the world and not covet the part played by those better-equipped to be our leading lights.

My ambitions have always been very modest, which is perhaps a blessing. I have many times achieved my ambitions precisely because they were so modest – even if, at the time of conception, they seemed far out of reach. I remember my very first: to own a bicycle. This was realised even before I left school, by the purchase – for the magnificent sum of 12 shillings and sixpence, industriously saved by putting 150 weeks' of Saturday's penny into a tin box – of a second-hand lady's machine with a larger front wheel than rear. At that moment, I thought that anybody who needed them could have all the rest of the things in the world.

Yet it wasn't very long before I grew dissatisfied with this machine and began casting envious glances at boys with better ones: all chromium plate and glossy paint. I set my heart on a Raleigh Light Roadster with three-speed gears, displayed by the local cycle agent in his shop window. That one, and no doubt very many more, were sold from his shop before I finally rode down the high street with a heart singing for joy, upon my very own.

Motorcycles were the inevitable next step after push-bicycles, but when it became necessary for me to buy one, at age twenty, having got a job with a wholesale milk company at their Heathfield depot, seven miles away, I hadn't a penny in the world. Father very kindly sent me £12 and 10 shillings and I was able to purchase the machine of my choice. Unfortunately, just as I was about to pay him back the last instalment of his money, I damaged the machine very badly in an accident – landing myself back in debt again.

A friend who was riding pillion and I both finished that very lovely Sunday by the sea in hospital at Eastbourne. In the course of a lifetime, even a short life, most of us have a brief encounter with death; some of us, many such encounters. This was my first. Having ridden the trusty little machine up a 10ft embankment before promptly somersaulting with it back down onto the road, I still marvel at my getting away with a cut eyebrow and slight concussion. My friend didn't get off so lightly: three weeks in hospital, to my three days.

My next ambition cost me £93, which meant borrowing £50 from my mother. It was a motorcycle and combination, a brand new Rudge Special with a Watsonian Cabin Cruiser sidecar. After twelve months, I sold it for £30, having acquired yet another ambition: a sportscar. It was a long, low, powerful little Singer, and at his first inspection my father sardonically branded it 'another folly'. The name stuck; she was 'The Folly' until I very reluctantly parted with her at a handsome profit after World War Two, having driven her for 25,000 trouble- and accident-free miles.

But she was still in my possession when Sir Thomas Inskip indicated in the House of Commons on 30th May 1938 that the government had made plans to provide for universal national service in time of war. The world's heart had stopped beating as it stood by as if petrified and watched Hitler's armies overrun Austria, and again upon Hitler's defiant announcement on 13th March that the federal state of Austria was dissolved and that the country was now annexed to the mighty German Empire. But I, like millions of others, preferred to ignore the ominous rumblings of distant thunder. I was still living in the sunshine, and the storm would not pass my way. I had my little Sports Singer, my newly acquired puppy named Barry and after one or two very brief and very mild flirtations, Renee was the girl of the moment. Life was at last being a little kinder to me.

SEVEN

After a hard day's work at one of our milk depots, either Glynde, on the slopes of the South Downs, or Etchingham, I drove quickly home, had tea, washed, shaved, put on my best clothes, and awaited the arrival of Renee. She and I would wander arm in arm down our lane, up to the windmill and follow the bridlepath, known as the red road, down into Rotherdale, Barry all the while searching for rabbits in the undergrowth, among the woods and hedges, only occasionally popping out to make sure he hadn't lost us.

My friendship with Renee was a very uncertain affair, and probably unsatisfactory to us both. I had known her for quite some time by this point, as she had been working at one of the big houses where I was very friendly with the dear old lady occupier. I worked there too, with a regular contract to tend the lawns during the summer months.

This job was quite a pleasure to me, not only because of the lovely surroundings, but specifically because the lawns – which included a croquet pitch, double tennis court and rose garden – set the garden off perfectly when neatly mown. My job gave me a sense of possession as part of this lovely garden, and I was free to wander in at random and mow this or that piece of grass at any time during the cool of the evening.

What is more soothing than to work in a beautiful, flower-scented garden in the evening after a busy, noisy day? There is perfect quiet, tranquillity, beauty, the marvellous aroma of shrubs and flowers, a feeling of being at peace with the world, set apart from all that is artificial and worldly and unclean. A writer once said you are nearer God's heart in a garden than anywhere else on Earth. Is that true? Nearer than when kneeling in prayer at church or at the graveside of a loved one, or when lying in bed in old age waiting for death to come? Yes, I rather think so.

Perhaps it has to do with the temperament of the person. I don't know, and I'm opposed to generalising about anything, but I do know that when I am enjoying a quiet evening stroll through a garden or flower-spangled woods or parks or countryside, a certain mood settles upon me. I reflect and begin to count my blessings and think how good it is to be alive. I begin to feel more well-disposed towards people, even those whom I don't much like, even my enemies and people who've not treated me very well. One can often find the solution to life's more difficult problems just by taking a quiet evening stroll through a garden or countryside. The very atmosphere of peace and tranquillity allows one to view a problem from an entirely different perspective, attack it from a different angle.

In this garden, I began to acquire a new outlook upon life. The tennis courts were hidden from the house by the foliage of beautiful copperbeech and pine trees. They may not have been good for the lawn but the trees created a lovely shady seclusion along the top of the steep grass bank that led down to the courts. There we had stood, Renee and I, one hot summer's evening. I could feel the perspiration coursing down my back, hot from my exertions pushing the mower swiftly across and across the tennis courts. She had hailed me from the top of the bank, and I had been very glad of an excuse to stop work for a moment.

It was a good deal cooler under the trees, and the breeze felt cold on my wet skin. I pulled on my jacket for fear of catching a chill as Renee called out.

"Aren't you nearly through with pushing that silly old thing across and across the lawn?"

"Well, no," I replied. "I've quite a bit more to do yet."

"You won't even get it done by dark?"

"Oh, I think so."

"I want you to come up and have some supper with me."

"Oh, I don't think I ought to do that. Won't Mrs Dalesworthy mind?"

"She won't even know about it, my dear boy. She's away for a few days."

"Well, if you won't get into trouble."

I hurried and finished the lawn, a little excited. Renee was waiting for me at the top of the gardens with tea and salad sandwiches beautifully laid out on trays on the beech path in front of the music room. It was my first intimate encounter with Renee; until now, we'd only ever exchanged a cursory hello/goodnight. Now, here I was, in this very pleasant scene, studying her. I've never been very good at conversation, and in the presence of this conspicuously attractive young lady, I sensed myself becoming more tongue-tied than usual. For quite a while, I contributed very few words except yes and no. Palpably struggling to draw me out, Renee grew bored, and blurted out: "Dick, when are you going to stop being a smug, complacent fool?"

I was severely shaken. "I don't know what you mean, I'm afraid."

She was quiet for a moment. "Do you think me so very unattractive?"

"No, no, of course not. In fact, I think you're very nice."

"Very nice? Ha, ha!" She pulled her already short dress further up her thighs. "Do you think I've got very pretty legs?"

She had, certainly. I said nothing and tried to keep my eyes averted.

"Well?"

"Yes, they're very lovely, Renee."

She got up and walked to the rose pergola at the top of the steps that led down to the rose borders and stood there, one hand on the latticework. I walked over and stood behind her. She turned to me and I saw she was crying.

"What's wrong, Renee?" I had no idea.

She toyed with the last remaining button on my jacket, and I took a dirty handkerchief – the only one I had – from my pocket and wiped her eyes.

"Renee, what have I done to cause these?"

"You haven't done anything, Dick."

"Well, then, what have I said?"

"No, you've not said anything either. It's just that I'm a fool, Dick. I'm a damned little fool. Don't bother about me."

We stood very close and I put an arm around her waist and pulled her very gently towards me. She turned her tear-stained face towards mine and looked wildly into my eyes. For years to come, that first passionate kiss would haunt me like a murder on my conscience.

EIGHT

It was not easy to say goodbye to my mother and father. I had by this time done several raids on the Ruhr and Rhine, Westphalia regions of western Germany, and it was pretty easy to see that it was just a question of time. Many crews got it on their very first trip; some managed three, others as many as five. Others still completed their first tour of ops and then went back to training for a rest before resuming ops. Sooner or later, they all got it. Germany was defending her cities extremely well.

With these facts weighing heavy on my heart, I sat down at the kitchen table. It was the last morning of my leave, my last such morning for many years. This was indeed goodbye; I felt it. Mother had been up and cooked me a glorious breakfast of porridge and eggs and bacon, rounded off with my usual slice of bread and marmalade – a habit I adhere to whenever humanly possible. I kissed my mother tenderly and thanked God that she bore me up so very bravely and did not cry. The sight of her tears would have broken my heart. I shook hands with my father looking him squarely in the eyes, striving to convey no fear. It didn't work. He read in my eyes – he confided years later – the certain knowledge that I wasn't coming back.

The nine o'clock train rumbled over the arch straddling Rotherfield Lane where I had played cricket as a boy with my cousin Eric. It panted its way up the incline out of Mayfield and I nodded farewell to my favourite haunts as we slid past Myles field and the nuns' fields, under the Tunbridge Wells Road and the white bridge, my mind registering swiftly and indelibly this last picture of the scenes of my boyhood and the romances of my manhood, which I was to treasure in my heart for five desperate years, and which would, like an old photograph, grow very, very dim as time passed but never quite fade out.

Connie sat opposite me. She too was returning to duty. Her attempts at brightness were tragic. Both of us knew what was going on in the other's heart.

"I'm so dreadfully afraid that one night you won't come back. The agony I suffer when I hear him say, 'One of our aircraft is missing'."

We drew out away from my familiar landscape.

"Did you remember to pack those oranges Auntie sent up for you, Ricky?"

"Yes, I've got them in my small case. Old Hooker will be after me tonight when he knows I've got them. He loves oranges, you know. I shall have one tonight all peeled and quartered on my locker beside my bed; I'll eat it as I read myself to sleep."

"Anything else on your locker beside your bed, Ricky?"

"Well, yes," I replied mischievously. "There's a dressing mirror, a bottle of ink, two or three pens, a pencil, two pipes, a camera, a German-English dictionary."

"And loads and loads of photographs?"

"And one photograph of a very lovely girl sitting on a sergeant's wireless operator's coat on the banks of the Cam."

"Oh, Ricky," she broke down.

I crossed over, sat beside her and took her hands in mine.

"Connie, my darling, this won't do at all. Dry those tears and smile for me. Look, the world's still beautiful. They're getting the hay in over there. There are cows in the fields and ducks on the ponds, and the sun's shining, and it's a lovely day, and the war is miles away. I'll come down to Cambridge again my next leave; perhaps one weekend before if I can manage it. You've got such lovely surroundings there, Connie. No wonder Rupert Brooke wrote poetry about it. You've barely shown me anything of it yet, you know. After all, we only had one weekend to, well, to do everything."

"I wonder if we'll ever have another, Ricky."

"Of course – we'll have many others. We've a whole life before us, haven't we? We shall drift down the river in our canoe again, or should I say up the river? We shall go all the way up to Grantchester from Magdalene College. I should love passing all those beautiful old buildings, gliding silently under the willows. Think of it, Connie: a sunny day, a canoe, you and me, and the river. Magdalene

College, Great Bridge, St John's College, St John's Bridge, Trinity College, Trinity Bridge, Clare College, Clare Bridge."

"You're doing very well, Ricky, but haven't you forgotten something?"

"Er, have I?"

"You didn't mention the Bridge of Sighs."

"Oh, yes! Built in 1826 at St John's College, named after the bridge connecting the Doge's Palace and the prison in Venice."

"You needn't ever be out of work. You've got a memory like an elephant."

"I'm just proving to you, dear, that I did read that book you sent me."

"All right. You've got as far as Clare Bridge. What do we do now?"

"Well…" I tried to look wicked. "As there are still quite a lot of people about, we continue on down – up, yes, up, so sorry – up the river past King's College, under King's Bridge, Queen's College, Queen's Bridge, and out into the Granta and into the meadows. And then we'll tie up somewhere, disembark and lie down under the trees and you shall play me all of your favourite records, commencing with *Liebesträume*."[13]

"Oh, Ricky, you make it seem so real and perfectly lovely."

"Oh, we haven't nearly finished yet. You must show me Byron's Pool and we shall have tea at the Red Lion."

"With honey for tea?"

---

13   *Liebesträume* (German for *Dreams of Love*) is a set of three solo piano works by Hungarian composer Franz Liszt, published in 1850.

"And then we'll see if the clock is still stopped at ten to three."[14]

She stood up and took her case from the luggage rack. I started searching my pockets for the tickets – I never remember which pocket I put them in. We stood facing each other as the train jerked to a halt, and we clutched each other to maintain our balance. After pushing our way through to the barrier, we took the underground without speaking. We parted at Bank, she for Liverpool Street, and I for King's Cross. As I kissed her on the crowded platform, she gave me one of her half-smiles. Tears stung my face.

"Goodbye, Ricky. Write often."

The doors glided across in front of her pale face, and I stood with my hand raised to my cap in military salute, smiling, but my heart miserable. I turned away before the last coaches had passed me and made my way upstairs.

---

14   This is a reference to Rupert Brooke's poem 'The Old Vicarage, Grantchester', written in Berlin in 1912, which ends: 'Deep meadows yet, for to forget/The lies, and truths, and pain?. . . oh! yet/Stands the Church clock at ten to three?/And is there honey still for tea?'

Richard (centre) with his brothers Raymond (left) and Harry, in Mayfield, East Sussex, c.1939.

NINE

Back in the aerodrome, my room seemed cold and cheerless though it was a hot day. I picked up the photograph and looked at it for several minutes, then sat down and began writing to her. Before I got far, Hooker came in. He was a tonic to everybody: bright and breezy, and always laughing, he had an inimitable way of getting himself out of any trouble his careless, happy-go-lucky manner got him into.

"Hello Dickie. Back, then? Had a good time? Seen the noticeboard? You're on tonight, you know. Johnny Brooks has had it, so's Sammy Yeoman and Cheeseman. Still haven't heard anything of Beard. We're the last of the old Brightonians now, Dickie. I've put your guns on and checked your gear. You hadn't got any spare valves, so I put two in the pocket above the oxygen. Here's your mail: Brighton, Southampton, Tunbridge Wells, Cambridge – you're a dark horse, you know, you ol' sod. Oh look, Dickie,

I took ol' Blondie down to Lincoln last night and she said that that little dark one who was with us when we spilled that beer over that barmaid who you were sweet on – you know, in the Unicorn—"

"Did you say Johnny's gone?" I said quietly.

"Yeah, night before last. Bloody well shakes you, don't it? Wonder who's next, Dickie, you or me? We're the last of the old Brightonians, you know."

"Am I really on tonight?"

"Well, you was, but I got you off. I told Dickert you weren't back at four o'clock so he scrubbed you and put Donaldson on instead. You're posted, you know. Ol' King was as wild as hell about that letter you sent the CO."

I sat quiet for a moment.

"You ever thought anything about getting married, Les?" I said at last.

"Yes, quite a lot, but not on this bloody job, Dickie. Here today and gone tomorrow. Get your wife in the spud line and then you get it. If you're thinking about it, think for a long time, Dickie. Look at Yeoman, Brooks, Elterington, Tate, Bramfield, Derby, Smudge Smith. How do you suppose their wives feel? Bramfield, married a week; Smudge Smith, shot down the same day he married. If you've got your eye on anything special, Dickie, make her wait, or else get yourself off flying. There's plenty doing that, you know. Get yourself put in the glasshouse for 'lack of moral courage'. Christ, I'd rather die tonight." For once, he paused. "You serious?"

I was unpacking my suitcase. His eagle eye missed nothing.

"Oh, oranges, eh? Yes thanks, Dickie." He bit an enormous piece of the rind away with his fake teeth and chomped into the fruit as one would an apple. I wiped some of the juice from my tunic and red coverlet and eyed him balefully. He tossed the tattered remains of the orange into my fireplace. He was always a very contrary eater of oranges.

"Come on, let's go and get some tea." Hooker crashed out of the room and I followed him rather less boisterously. Donaldson wasn't back when we went to breakfast next morning. I had the feeling of being a cheat.

I went to bed early that night. I had been to report to my new flight commander after confessing that I had indeed been posted from 'A' flight to 'B' flight on account of my going over the head of 'A' flight commander to get my leave to correspond with Connie's holiday. Although this unfairness rankled in my mind, 'B' flight commander did his best to put me at ease and said that the usual dishonour of a flight posting did not apply in my case since the leave was my due and could have been arranged by 'A' flight commander had he been disposed to bother. This eased my mind considerably, and he handed over to me the sole responsibility of wireless and electrical equipment on Hampden aircraft 'J' for Johnnie; I was to be permanent wireless operator. This boosted my spirits considerably, as up to now I had been switched from one aircraft to another almost daily, giving me no chance to become accustomed to the habits of any particular crew or the peculiarities of any one set of radio equipment. This may not seem very important, but being unfamiliar with equipment can be disastrous. I myself was once called upon to take over an aircraft as wireless operator at the last minute.

We were to lay a magnetic mine between the islands and the mainland at La Rochelle. Our 'drome was up in the north of England, and as we came south for the west coast of France, we began to get into trouble with some of our own defence boys while passing over Hampshire. The captain ordered the colour recognition cartridge to be fired, and I automatically loaded the pistol with a cartridge from the first three in the rack, which would, I knew, be the correct colour for the first period of the night. I slid back my observation cowl and fired into the darkness. A couple of seconds later I was terrified to see the green stars light up above us. At the same instant, the captain's voice roared at me over the intercom: "Wireless operator, what the hell colours are you firing?"

In all the remaining cartridges in the rack, I had no red-green, the arranged recognition colour for the period up to midnight. Thankfully, it being early in the war, our AA defences, like our offences, were hopelessly inadequate, and we went on to lay our mine quite safely. Even so, that little incident created no small amount of unnecessary tension and action for the gun crews and population of the district below (doubtless an alert would have been sounded upon seeing our incorrect colour signal). That's to say nothing of the probability of a lucky shot destroying us in mid-air; the probability of the loss of a crew of four men upon whose training hundreds of pounds had been spent (at a time when we were pitifully short of trained aircrews); the probability of the loss of an aircraft costing the rate payer

£30,000; the probability of wrecked lives and property if our bomb-load and aircraft had fallen on a city.

On another occasion, while returning home, flying up across Germany, we were driven rather high by a warm patch of anti-aircraft fire and it was necessary to take the precaution of using oxygen. The responsibility of regulating the supply to pilot, rear gunner and wireless operator fell to the wireless operator, me, in whose cabin the bottles were stored (the navigator had his own). We had been using oxygen for barely ten minutes when the pilot asked me to turn up his supply a bit. Looking round at the oxygen meter, I was amazed to see it reading zero. I turned on another bottle and it too lasted only a few minutes before it was exhausted.

I turned off my own supply and went to turn on one of the last two bottles. Neither of the valves would budge, and they were not the sort you could hit with a hammer or unscrew with a spanner. They had a circular disc about two inches in diameter, with a milled outer cage that one could only operate by hand or with a great pair of Stillson grips. The bottles were, of necessity, crammed in among other equipment, making it impossible to apply more than thumb and finger to the valve.

The pilot and I recovered consciousness only once we had dropped to a lower altitude. The rear gunner said he hadn't known anything about it, as he had been asleep all the time. It was yet another incident that could have meant the loss of an aircraft and four lives, and it had occurred as a direct result of my transfer to an aircraft without having time to acquaint myself fully with its equipment. No doubt all these snags were being faced by other squadrons in all the services. In fighting the Battle of Britain, our tiny air force and hopelessly inadequate anti-aircraft defences were locked in a life-or-death struggle with the entire might of the German Luftwaffe, whose supply of men and machines seemed inexhaustible. Day after day in that lovely August of 1940, our tiny forces challenged the enemy over the countryside of Kent and Sussex in a cloudless summer sky.

Of course, we saw little of this tucked away up in the north of England in our bomber 'dromes. The only noises keeping us awake were those made by our own aircraft. Lying in bed that first night back on duty, I reflected on my seven days' leave just ended. What a lot we had crammed in. Every night it had been after midnight before I'd climbed into bed, and even now I can remember pausing in front of my dressing mirror, looking myself in the eye, and saying, "My God, how tired and haggard you look." Each night I would resolve to have an early night tomorrow, but each tomorrow brought me closer to Connie and closer to our final goodnight.

Now that our time together was over, I was rather glad she had upheld such high moral principles. I had imparted from her letters that she had some very firm ideas about premarital sex and relationships, and I held many of the same ideas myself. Our difference was, I thought that if two people had definite plans to marry and were indeed sufficiently in love, then that was the right time to experience each other, to confirm that they were well suited. Not that my thoughts were at all centred on Connie on that last evening under the tree on the knoll; I was thinking of my own physical satisfaction. The letter I received from her a few days later proved how very right I was not to destroy those high ideals she carried in her heart.

I began to think more seriously of marriage. Yet things seemed so unreal and the future so dreadfully uncertain. 'Not on this bloody job, Dickie,' Hooker had said. 'If you've got your eye on anything special, make her wait or else get yourself off flying.' Why should I do either of these things? Why shouldn't she and I take life in both hands just for a little while? Why shouldn't I go down to Cambridge on my very next weekend and have a two-day honeymoon at the Red Lion in Grantchester?

TEN

Life on the aerodrome had not changed in my brief absence
except to become busier, noisier, more alert and more
dangerous. Fresh aircrews had come and gone. Many faces
once well known were missing, and many new ones had
taken their place. Brand new aircraft took the place of lost
aircraft, with modifications giving greater efficiency. Most
machines now had automatic pilot and shoring landing
equipment, with Marconi radios replacing the old T1082
and R1083. Our routine was much the same: take-off at
dusk, home by about 6.30am, bed till noon, then breakfast,
and afternoon and evening off, unless maximum effort
was ordered by No. 5 Group HQ for some special target.[15]
After an operation, all machines would be overhauled,
and if a member of the crew wanted to test a piece of

15   No. 5 Group was a Royal Air Force bomber group.

equipment – provided time allowed and the captain could get the crew together – we would do an 'air test' (or DI, Daily Inspection, as we used to call them). Lunch was at one o'clock, followed by a smoke and a chat over coffee and a newspaper in the luxurious lounge adjoining the sergeants' quarters.

The conscientious wireless operator and air gunner would then repair to the gun-room or armoury where his twin VGO machine guns were stored. He would completely disassemble and reassemble the gun, leaving it beautifully cleaned and oiled, before commandeering a 'gharrie' – that is, a transport wagon, usually driven by the WAAF[16] – to get his guns taken out to his particular machine.

For the straight AG (air gunner only), when he has fixed his guns and checked his ammunition pans, he has finished till briefing time at 6pm. But for the WO-AG (wireless operator-air gunner) who has acquired the position of First Operator, he must again check his transmitter, receiver and oxygen. This involves calling up one or two stations for frequency check and calling up Base Control on the RT (broadcast) set, the latter being very important in the event of having to land in fog. I spent many anxious afternoons out in 'J' for Johnnie checking and rechecking as best I knew how all the electrical equipment that was, I knew, the very lifeline to which we would cling all night on our charge out over the North Sea and down into Germany.

---

16 The Women's Auxiliary Air Force, the female auxiliary of the Royal Air Force during World War Two.

I remember the tremendous heat, the perspiration pouring out of me as I sat under the perspex cowl quoting "Hello Decka control, hello Decka control, this is Decka aircraft J for Johnnie calling, this is Decka aircraft J for Johnnie, are you receiving me, please, are you receiving me? Over to you, over."

I remember too how relieved I was to hear Decka control's response confirming it was receiving me loud and clear. Rarely did this assurance come upon the first attempt; usually considerable juggling with the frequency was needed, it having been left offset after the previous night's operations. Machines being in such short supply, they had to be flown every night if flying conditions were good, provided they could be kept reasonably serviceable.

Once dubiously satisfied, and having walked the twenty to thirty minutes back from my aircraft, my next job was to acquire a parachute – which were in dreadfully short supply. Our sister squadron had recently moved to a 'drome a few miles south, taking the lion's share of parachutes with them. Some old stagers, that is to say, the Regulars,[17] had their own personal chute, which they guarded preciously, but we new boys were at our wits' end to know where to get fixed up with one, even when we knew for sure we were flying that night.

The obvious first place to look was the parachute store. On the way there, I ran into Hooker.

"Hello Dickie. Where're you going?"

"Trying to get a parachute."

---

17   A Regular is a full-time soldier, as opposed to a reservist.

"Are you on tonight, then?"

"I don't know. The lists aren't up yet. But I expect I shall be. Wasn't on last night, you see."

"No, I know." He fell into step beside me. "You could have mine, if I'd got one."

"Yes, I guess so, but you haven't, so don't talk daft."

"I don't know if Redman's going on tonight. He's a good scout. He'll lend you his if he's not flying. Lent it to me last night, bless him. Christ, Dickie, what a furnace. Hope you're not on that tonight."

I hoped so too. Hooker's aircraft had staggered home minus a lot of parts. It wasn't uncommon. We were losing a lot of aircraft lately.

"Got a chute for tonight, Corporal?" I asked upon arrival at the parachute store.

"News travels pretty fast it, don't it, Serg. Who told you they were in?"

"Nobody," I replied. "You mean to say you've actually got a serviceable parachute in your parachute store?"

"I've brand new ones, just come in. Need unpacking, but you can have this one by six o'clock – and keep quiet about it."

I chucked half a crown on the bench and gave him my name and number.

"Pack it so it will open," I quipped as we walked out. Before the night was out, I would know for certain that he had.

We walked on through the 'drome and out of the main gates. Hooker was perspiring freely as he swaggered along beside me, telling me of Spain's latest exploits, throwing back his head in great roars of laughter, and all the while chomping down toffees – of which he seemed to have an endless supply distributed about his person. I let him do all the talking; his boisterous remarks seldom needed a reply. I was thinking deeply. After tonight, tomorrow, Friday, I was leaving for a long weekend. I was going down to Cambridge.

Just one more flight.

Time carried forward— 795.85 / 00.30

Date	Hour	Aircraft Type and No.	Pilot	Duty	Remarks (including results of bombing, gunnery, exercises, etc.)	Flying Times Day	Night
16/8/40	2055	4372.4 Hampden	P/O Hynes	1st Operator	OPERATIONS. AS DETAILED		8.40
18/8/40	1205	4372.4 Hampden	Sgt. Kneller	1st Operator	A/c CALIBRATION TEST.	1.45	
19/8/40	1206	4372.4 Hampden	P/o Hynes	1st Operator	TEST.		
21/8/40	2130	4372 Hampden	P/o Hynes	1st Operator	OPERATIONS. FAILED TO REACH TARGET		6.06
24/8/40	2245	4372 Hampden	P/o Hynes	1st Operator	OPERATIONS. AS DETAILED		7.10
26/8/40	1035	4372 Hampden	P/o Hynes	1st Operator	NORTH SEA SEARCH	3.30	
26/8/40	2150	4372 Hampden	P/o Hynes	1st Operator	OPERATIONS. AS DETAILED		6.35
29/8/40		4373 Hampden	P/o Hynes	1st Operator	SHOT DOWN OVER TARGET.		

WITHDRAWN FROM AIR CREW DUTIES.

TOTAL TIME

LETTERS HOME

Location unspecified

September 1st, 1940

My dear mother, father & brothers & sisters,

I expect you will know long before you receive this that I am a prisoner of war. However, I can assure you all that it is not so bad after all, and I am fit and well and unhurt, having escaped from our machine safely by parachute. This is only my second day here but I am already settling down and making myself quite at home. We are all RAF chaps here, and are being treated with the utmost respect. I share a room with my rear gunner and another pilot; it is a very cosy and warm room, and the entire camp is very nice, with beautiful surroundings. The food is very good and there is enough for everyone. Nobody goes hungry.

I expect the Red Cross will have given you all the news as to what you may and may not send to me but some fags and tobacco, some clean laundry, a pair of boots, a pullover, toothpaste and toothbrush, hairbrush, chocolate, matches, a pipe and things like that will be very welcome if you would be good enough to send some of them. But the Red Cross will send me quite a lot of things I expect, so you will be able to see what they are sending first. I have met some of my old pals here, but this being for air forces, I have not seen A or E.[18]

I do ask you all not to be unhappy because of this; being a prisoner of war is quite good fun really. I have already seen some very beautiful country; and as I say, it is very lovely here. Please let all my friends know that I am OK, especially Connie. Please write to her, Mother, won't you, and try to keep her chin up for me. I have written her a card, which I shall send same time as this but I shall not be able to get through to you very often. I shall expect lots of letters, tho, so I hope people will write to me. I expect Les Hooker will have written to you. Please let him know where I am and that I am OK.

It is nice and hot here today, and I have been lying out all morning in the sun, as of course we have no work to do. It was lovely out there. A pretty young German girl even came into the field to milk the sheep. Boy, was I thrilled! All the people I have met have been awfully nice to me.

I'm growing a lovely beard, so I expect that by the time I get a razor I shall be past shaving.

Hope you are all keeping OK and well. Don't worry about me, Mother, I am quite well and having a good time. Give my love to all, and if Leslie hasn't written to the

---

18   'A or E' refers to two relatives who were serving in the army.

people in my address book which he will have found in my drawer, would you do that for me, Mother? Just let them know where I am and so on.

Hope to be home pretty soon, but in the meantime, keep smiling and don't worry.

Send me a few things when you can, but get in touch with the Red Cross first. One more thing, Mother: It is Connie's birthday on Nov 30, so if I'm not home, please buy her an enamelled brush, comb and mirror set in blue, and send it to her from me.

And now I must close, sending my love to all.

Your loving son,

Dick.

Location unspecified

Boxing Day, 1940

My dear mother, father, brothers and sisters and Connie,

I write comprehensively to you all, this Boxing Day 1940, once again to assure you of my well-being, and to say how very much I hope you have all enjoyed your Christmas. Of course I flatter myself sufficient to think that my shining countenance has been missed just a wee bit from the happy throng, but I sincerely trust not too much so as to damp your spirits; and I hope you all had a very happy time. As for us, well, we have had a remarkably pleasant time, under the circumstances. We had our rooms decorated with holly, streamers and some very pretty foliage of pine; we were allowed beer and wine, had cigarettes, a Christmas pantomime, and bags of sing-songs. We missed only our dear ones at Home Sweet Home and the food.

Incidentally, they tell me I was trying to stand on my head on a stool at 3 o'clock this morning but all I've got to say to that is that if I was trying to, then I bet I did, at least, retain all my drinks and eats: and I'm fresh as a daisy again tonight. I have received a parcel from Geneva, but Red Cross parcels are not coming through and Geneva are sending us more. Now I send my best wishes and love to you all and 'Here's to next Christmas'.

Yours,

Dick.

Kreigsgefangemenlager des Luftwaffe, Gr. III

Sunday, January 19th, 1941

My dearest mother,

Sunday evening and again, as ever, my thoughts ride back along the 'trail o'winding', to the land of my dreams, as the song says. I picture you toddling off to your little Mission Hall as usual (posting my letter on the way). I picture you inside, praying as you do each Sunday for the safe return of the loved ones. I picture you chatting with Aunt Herry discussing my latest letter. I picture your return home to find Chummie smoking by the fire (dear old Chummie),[19] reading the Sunday paper (it used to be the *Sunday Circle* from Mrs Wickenden). And I expect he peers over his specs, says 'Well', eats his bun, drinks his wine, lights his pipe, says 'Where's little 'un?', toddles outside, and then off to bed; and that's the end of another day. God bless you both, Mother.

---

19 'Chummie' was Richard's pet name for his father, Alfred Wicker.

No words of mine can tell how glad I am to get your letters (3 up to now), 13 all told. I am afraid I have caused you an awful lot of work and worry, Mother, but you will only say, ''Tis a pleasure to do what we can'. Many thanks for sending parcel. You have sent just the things I need most and it should reach me middle of Feb. Bands with socks, slippers, handkerchiefs and pair of plimsolls next time. I shall then have everything I need, so fill up with choc. Received some fags and fourth food parcel from Red X last week. Ask Auntie and Tillie to send my regards to A & E. Very sorry to hear of Uncle Harry. Have no patience with Alfred Miles.[20] The country has enough expense without unnecessary wives' and widows' pensions. Still – many thanks to Phyllis for the letter. Tell her, yes, I still retain my title of Mr Clever.

Goodbye for now, and my thanks and best wishes to everyone.

Your loving son,

Dick.

---

20 The Miles family were neighbours of the Wickers in Mayfield, East Sussex.

Christmas 1941, in Barth, north–east Germany. Richard is third from left.

Stalag Luft 2[21]

Friday, June 6th, 1941

My dear mother,

Am glad to say I received my second parcel from you on the 19th last month, the contents of which I have found most useful indeed and I must thank you very, very much for everything, and the care and trouble taken in your selection of articles, and for all that you and many others are doing for me. I have not eaten the 'special' chocolate yet but it looks very tempting. I can do with lots of that and also Lifebuoy Soap.

The letters from Ruth, Phyllis and yourself, written on my birthday arrived together on Monday 2/6/41 this week, and I am glad to see you all write in cheerful strain. Please tell Ruth. Have not heard from the people in Switz yet, but mail comes in pretty regularly now, so no doubt I shall hear pretty soon. I have a good many letters lately, total to date, 133. Elsie still leads the field with 25 to her credit, Amy 15, yourself, Ruth and Connie 11, Raybo and Phyll 7, Ruby 9, and the rest from Fred, Harry, etc. and many good friends including two from Maggie Miles.[22] I hope nobody will feel hurt if I fail to reply often or mention their letters, as my paper fills all too quickly. Nobody sends photos but I shall expect snaps in every letter from now on, as I am about the only one in the room without them, altho I still lead the field in our 'mail Derby'.

---

21   Stalag Luft II was a POW camp near Litzmannstadt (now Łódź) in Poland.

22   Richard lists letters received from his eight siblings, Fred, Harry, Ray (whom he also called 'Billie'), Phyllis, Elsie, Ruth, Lily and Daisy, as well as from girlfriends Connie, Amy and Ruby.

Red X food and cig parcels are coming in better now, but some cig and tobacco parcels do not arrive. Don't send any more until I pay.

Our grand 'Sports Day' went off very well but I'm ashamed to say I won nothing, altho I leaped 15 feet in the long jump and galloped well in the three-legged. The summer has arrived now, and I do lots of sunbathing and am keeping remarkably fit. The chap in the room received a dartboard recently, so Pop had best look out for himself when I return.

Now I must close, sending my fondest love to you, Mother dear, and to Chummie.

Your ever loving son,

Richard.

Stalag Luft I[23]

Monday, December 1st, 1941

My dearest mum and dad,

I send you, my brothers and sisters and my friends my best wishes for Christmas and the New Year. But I suppose that you at home, same as we are here, will be facing this Christmas, as last, with very mixed feelings, since we cannot ignore Christmas and yet it is very different to work up much enthusiasm over it, things being as they are. However, in case you should imagine us gazing moodily into the fire, head in hands, pining vainly for the good times we have previously known, I should like straight away to set your mind at rest, because we shall certainly not be hungry or

---

23   Stalag Luft I was a POW camp near Barth, Western Pomerania, Germany.

thirsty, and we are organising 2 or 3 concerts over Christmas while in our rooms during the evenings; we shall have lots of musical interludes from various people playing mouth organs, whistle pipes, concertinas and piano-accordions; and everybody, whether they like it or not, will have to contribute a song, dance, or recitation, so I've no doubt we shall have a comparative 'good time'.

I only hope that things will not be slowed up too much at home, and that Christmas will go over big in the good old English fashion in spite of everything and that by next year we shall be together again. So much for that.

Now, Mother, please convey my very best wishes to Aunt May. I am very sorry to hear of her trouble, and hope her foot gets well very, very quickly. Also hope that Ruth's little Micky is quite well again now, and that Tommie and all the other young folk, Harry's little girls, Fred's little Mary and young Lanie, are well, and going to have a swell time this Christmas, because I know how very much I used to look forward to it. I am still exceedingly fit and pray God that you Mother, and you Dad, are equally so; and send my thanks to all who have written to me during the year, as they have brought me much pleasure and consolation.

My very best wishes to you all.

Your ever loving son,

Dick.

Stalag Luft I
Saturday, January 10th, 1942

Dear Mother Mine,

I suppose that as the years roll by and we get older, we like to ignore rather than celebrate our birthday. But I am purposely writing your letter on Jan 10 so that I can wish you many 'Happy Returns of the day' and, though I don't suppose for a minute that this day, as I write, has been a particularly happy one for you, knowing as I do how you worry over we 'young devils' kicking about in various parts of the world, I do sincerely hope that you haven't had too many callers today ('just when you'd got a cake in the oven'), that the milk didn't boil over for once, and that you beat Chummie up at shove-ha'penny. Then you will at least have had a 'fairly' good day.

By the way, no one has written reminding me it's your birthday today, so I reckon it's pretty smart of me to remember, don't you?

Well, Mumsie, I expect you'd give a lot to skip over the years and find yourself a gay, irresponsible young lass working for Mr Henry Holder again, with an attractive young Alfred to come and take you out in the evening, but tonight you can at least sit back and say with truth, 'Well, I have done my bit to be a good wife and a good mother'. And when you make up your mind to leave us, we shall be able to say of you those words I have heard somewhere, 'My mother, she was good to her children and her God'.

Yes, you're a pretty wonderful person, Mother, and I hope your worries will soon be vanished in a happy reunion of us all, so that we can together celebrate our 'Many Happy Returns'.

Now: I received first mail of the year yesterday. All were sent in November, 2 were from you, dated 18th and 23rd (latest so far); 1 from Amy; 1 from Ruth; 1 from Connie; 1 from Puss (please thank her for writing, and tell Auntie I'll be after that wine pretty soon) & a Christmas card from Ruby. I cannot comment on your letters today, but I've had a lot from you lately, Mother (easily 1 a week), and have received all the photos OK & the cutting of Daisy's wedding, but in future, don't take my coat on wet Sunday evenings, take the 'Folly' [Richard's car].

Your ever loving son,

Dick.

Stalag Luft 3[24]

March 5th, 1943

Dear Mother o' Mine,

I had just finished reading the bit on the contents of my Oct parcel, in your letter of Jan 9th, on Monday, the 1st, when I had a package dumped onto my bed, and lo and behold, there's the parcel. I shall come back to that again in a moment, because I want to tell you of a very funny thing that happened at dinner the other day. My friend put my dinner bowl in front of me and said, 'There you are, try that,', to which I, being politely brought up, replied 'Thank you'.

---

24 Stalag Luft III was a POW camp near Sagan, Lower Silesia, Germany (now Żagań, Poland). A mass escape of seventy-six prisoners from this camp on the night of March 24/25th, 1944, became known as 'The Great Escape'. All but three of the escapees were recaptured, and fifty were subsequently executed.

'Oh don't thank me,' he went on, 'thank Providence,' and I said, 'Yes, we should thank the Lord' and then I saw poor old Mr Thomas presiding over a Baptist Chapel Sunday School treat, saying his usual Grace, 'We thank Thee Lord for this our food, And more because of Jesus's Blood, Preserve us Lord, and grant that we may feast in Paradise with Thee.' As I haven't heard that since my Sunday school days, I think that's pretty good, don't you?

Well, I was very pleased with the parcel, Mumsie, but then I always am, as they are always very good parcels. The shirts will do fine, and as usual, the liberal supply of 'Nutty' was most welcome. My mates can't make out where you get the milk chocolate, and I say, 'I don't know – she just gets it.'

Have been very lucky for cig parcels since writing last – 2 of 500 cigs from Grampie, 1 of 500 and 1 of 200 from you, 200 from United Dairies, 300 from Ruby, and 150 and ¼lb tobak from British Legion Mayfield. Had 3 books too, from Christine Knowles, but they're not worth mentioning – just trash. It was very nice for you to have the girls up for Christmas, as I'm sure they brightened things up for you quite a bit. Elsie, by the way, had sauce enough to tell me there were lots of dances on over Christmas, but she didn't take you [because] although you are still 'a gay girl', she thought 'jitterbugging a bit out of your line'. Whatever next! – I reckon you could jitterbug with the rest of us, eh? Sure you could.

I got a letter from Billie the day before yesterday written on Dec 14. Quite a cheery letter, with a nice bit of news, and telling me as how he and Harry hoped to meet at Christmas, as I now know, of course, that they did. I am so very, very glad to know they are more or less together out there. How nice, isn't it?

And here's the inevitable bottom of the page again, just when I've got into my stride, so I must send you lots of love, a big kiss and very many thanks for everything.

Your ever loving son,

Dick.

Stalag Luft 3

Sunday, March 21st, 1943

My dear mother,

Having been in a quandary all the week as to which of my sweethearts I should send this letter to, I have at last decided to send it to the most gracious of them all – my mother. Well, it is Sunday evening here, and about 20 minutes past 6, so altho I know your times to be very different to ours, nevertheless, I picture you at this moment toddling away over Fletchling St, probably just passing Dad's old home 'Rose Cottage' on your way to the Mission Hall. And in a little while, before I have finished writing this, probably, you will be inside, bowed in prayer, and I, unworthy as I am, shall be remembered in them. You may even sing the hymn, a very great favourite of mine (and I know it to be a great favourite of yours too, Mother) which was among ours at church this morning: 'I heard the voice of Jesus say, come unto Me, and rest'. It's as well to think about these words a bit in these times, isn't it? 'Lay down, thou weary one, lay down, Thy head upon My Breast.' Rather a lovely hymn altogether, I think – but I must go on to other things.

The accordion arrived safely on Friday 19th, and tho it is out of tune, and certainly you were robbed if you paid more than 30 bob for it, I found, when I took it into the wash house secretly at night, that I could work out my much loved signature tune 'Goodnight Sweetheart' every bit as sweetly and beautifully as ever I did (no nasty remarks from you, either, Phyllis). I played 'Little Valley in the Mountains', 'Isle of Capri, When April Sings', and one of these stupid modern things, 'Oh I Love the Kisses of Delores' quite well too, so altogether I'm really pleased with my little old bus, and I'm sure I'm going to enjoy myself with it immensely.

I was looking at my skates hanging beside my bed just now, and thinking I shall have to grease them and put them away for next season. It has been a very bad year for skating here, only four good skating days have we had, but during that period they were not still for a moment, so they have been well worth the trouble of sending out.

Talking of the weather, my face is already quite tanned by the Feb and March sun, quite hot it has been, and I look and feel exceedingly fit; in fact my friends here tell me I'm looking younger every day (but this might be to console me on my coming 30th birthday). Ah well. Goodnight, sweetheart, goodnight.

Your ever loving son,

Dick.

Stalag Luft 3

Sunday, May 7th, 1944

My dear mother,

Last month I received your letter Jan 22 and Feb 5 and 22. And yesterday I received 2 more dated Feb 12 and 19. I don't have anything special to talk about, except perhaps that I am pretty dejected at the time taken by our mail to reach each other these days. Considering that we pay Air Mail and Express charges, I think it deplorable that my letters to you take from 8 weeks to as many months to reach you, and that yours to me take from 2 to 4 months. We might almost as well not be corresponding at all. I had, of course, been wondering why you had not included the articles that I asked for in my last July letter in my parcels, until I received your letter yesterday of Feb 19, saying that you had only just received that letter.

█████████████████████████████████████
████████████████████████████████████ 25

In the place of photographs long unobtainable, I have managed to persuade a friend to do 2 little drawings of me, one of which I have sent to Connie, and the other I send with this letter. I do not say they are exactly me, but I believe they bear a strong resemblance. I don't always look as solemn as this, however. It is probably the boredom of sitting still for so long coming out (each of them took 2 hours).

I was quite amazed to see that old Chummie is 65 now. By jove, I've quite lost count of the years; I only realised a few days ago that I am 31 now. Heavens above and Moses in the bushes, I'll jolly soon be in my dotage 'when the years draw nigh when I shall say "I have no pleasure in them"'.

---

25   Two lines censored.

Postcard portait of Richard drawn by fellow POW in Stalag Luft
II, dated 22nd April 1944, enclosed with letter home dated 7th
May 1944, inscribed 'For Mother, from her loving son, Dick'

I am looking forward to the summer – the sun always lightens my heart considerably.

My love to you, Mother Dearest, and Chummie, the family and little chicks.

Your son,

Dick

Solingen, Germany[26]

Friday, May 4th, 1945

My dear mother,

I may race this letter to England but, as it may be a few days after my arrival [home] that I shall be able to get to you, I wish to say that I am free, and all is being done to get us home as soon as possible.

I was liberated on May 2nd, since which time I have been treated like a long-lost brother by the army chappies with whom I have come into contact.

Here where I arrived after a 150-kilometre-long ride from Lüneburg this afternoon, I have had good food and feel remarkably full for a change. This white bread tastes to me like cake (but that won't excuse you from making me some good old buns).

I cannot write a long letter here and now, as I am due to be examined for evacuation, but you may be sure that thoughts of home are very strong and my heart rejoices at the thought of seeing you, Dad and the rest pretty soon.

So goodbye for the time,

Your loving son,

Dick.

---

26 Solingen is a town in North Rhine-Westphalia, western Germany.

THE MARCH

It was the 19th April 1945 and we RAF prisoners of war had been evacuated from our camp M. Stammlager 357 at Fallingbostel eleven days earlier.[27] We had marched under heavy German guard around Lüneburg Heath to prevent the Allies from reclaiming us into their care. I had been shot down over Cologne on the night of 29th August 1940 and had lived on several POW camps in Germany and Poland. I was RAF POW 238.

Now at last we had passed single-file two miles long through an IRC barrier in a small village and had an American food parcel thrust into our hands.[28] Halted by the Germans in the shade of a long avenue of trees a few

---

27 Stammlager 357 (previously Stalag XI-D) was located just to the east of the town of Fallingbostel in Lower Saxony, north-western Germany.
28 The IRC is the International Rescue Committee, a humanitarian organisation, founded in 1933.

miles further on, we noticed plenty of aircraft in the sky, but we didn't mind – they were all ours. The Luftwaffe was grounded for lack of fuel.

My mate Harry Billett and I were eagerly opening our parcels and trying to decide what to start with. We'd had no food save a swede or sugar beet or some potatoes for ten days.

We paid no particular attention to a couple of RAF Typhoons buzzing around overhead, crossing and recrossing our columns.

I was just trying to smear some condensed milk on a biscuit when I happened to glance down the column to the archway of daylight formed by the trees and saw the two Typhoons swooping down upon us. I shouted, "Look out, Harry, they're coming in!" and dived for the ditch.

A second later, the first rocket exploded and I watched horrified as men were ripped apart screaming in agony. Frantically I clawed my way through a hedge and out into a field and ran. At the top of the field, five old German women were chasing a horse that had bolted and was spilling potatoes out of the back of its cart.

I ran on, panting and my heart pounding as the Typhoon came round again. Finally I fell to the ground exhausted, and realised all was quiet. I crept back to the roadway. Our New Zealander padre was moving about among the dead and wounded.

The final count was thirty-four RAF POW killed and over fifty seriously injured; seven German guards killed and fourteen injured. Five of my room-mates were gone: Hunt, Mackenzie, Joyce, Davie Bauldy, little Duffield, and also a good Kiwi friend of mine, Bill Watson, who on that day 19th April had completed five years' POW service.

At a post-war enquiry, it was found that no blame attached in any way to the pilots, since they plainly saw only the line of Germans on each side of our column, while we were almost entirely hidden by the trees.

LIBERATION

Diary notes, May 1945

Sunday, 6th May, 1945
Still here and a shocking wet morning. Saw my first English talkie last night. Just received orders to stand by for parade at 11.30 so may be on move.

Ex-POW embarkation camp, Borghorst, Germany [29]
Monday, 7th May, 10am
Moved out from Solingen on special transport (covered dodger) at 4pm yesterday. Covered just over 100 miles and arrived here at 9pm. The road was exceedingly difficult in places due to the recent shelling and bombing damage.

---

29   Borghorst (now called Steinfurt) is a town in North Rhine-Westphalia, north-west Germany.

Reconstruction goes on apace however, and it is really wonderful how quickly things are being put back into order by the army. Everywhere new bridges have had to be constructed, bomb and shell craters filled in, whole stretches of roads bypassed and new ones made, tons of debris – trees, tanks burned out, transport, etc., moved from the roads, all of which must have been a terrific task. A very great deal of war damage was in evidence.

Here we are billeted in the buildings of what was a German spinning factory, or whatever one should call a place where hemps and cottons and cat guts, etc., are produced and woven. Hundreds of loom machines lying still in orderly rows downstairs, while all around are tons and tons of bales of twine and cotton material of every description.

A large and airy building, lots of windows, wooden framed. Double-tier type bed, straw mattress and pillow and three beautiful, large, clean blankets made our arrival here a great joy. After a good old clean-up we were 'home'. What a novelty to sit down for 10pm supper. Sitting up to table is so jolly strange to us that I'm afraid we all felt a little self-conscious looking at each other across the table. And to be waited upon is, of course, quite unheard of. Another surprise was coming to us in the food. We had been told that a meal awaited us, so we all sat politely though impatiently waiting for it to be served up. In the meantime, we were supposed to make our meal of the biscuits and butter and jam already laid out. Once they realised, the boys sure went to town on those commodities, it being about 11pm, and having eaten nothing for 12 hours. The embarrassed orderlies could not possibly produce tea, biscuits, jam and butter fast enough, and soon the place was a mass of POWs running to and from the serving room with plates and pots of tea. The staff must have thought us more animal than human, and I guess they were right.

We don't quite know what happens to us here. Some lorry-loads of Indian troops left this morning for the airport. Unlike yesterday, it is a good flying day and it is said that a lot of groups will be taking off today, but whether it will get round to us or not, we don't know.

Later: 8.30pm

Well, they have not flown us home to England today, and there is absolutely nothing to indicate the probability of going at any time during the night. Over the radio in the hotel, I have just heard the announcement that Germany surrendered unconditionally at Gen Eisenhower's HQ at 02.41 today and that tomorrow will be celebrated as VE Day and Wednesday also will be a public holiday. This news was received coldly and unemotionally by everybody in the room, and probably will, of course, delay our departure another two days.

Here, I believe, they are doing their very utmost to starve us to death. The food, as I have said, is very good but there is not enough of it. I have no doubt the food problem is pretty difficult, but dammit, I've been hungry nearly five years; surely it's somebody else's turn now. I've just had my supper, which consisted of half a cup of tea. My four o'clock tea consisted of some beans in tomato, just the bottom of a tea plate covered, with bread and marg. Dinner was very nice indeed: steak and kidney pud with spuds and peas, but again all in very minute quantity. Lots of fellows I know went out and came in again, but this method of obtaining extra always strikes me as most deceitful. Having resisted resorting to it in much worse situations than these, I'm not going to start now.

The NAAFI canteen up in the town provides tea and biscuits,[30] but I was there at 7.30pm tonight and felt very disinclined to tag on to the end of a line of, I should say, 300 people, after all the queuing and lining up I've had to do for food in Germany. However, let me not grumble too much on this momentous day. The war with Germany is over, and it is quite time. The news has failed to move me in the slightest. I expect that is because of having had to sit back helplessly and watch for the greater part, cursing the government for not doing this, the army for not doing that, and the navy and air force for something else, and shouting continually, 'Why the hell don't they just put those bloody strikers against the wall?'

But when I look at it quietly and soberly, I realise that it has cost our nation, to say nothing of the cost to Russia and America, a terrific effort; and that in my heart I am glad and grateful to feel that the slaughter is over, and I myself a free man, though still in this godforsaken country. But let's see what tomorrow brings.

---

30   The NAAFI is the Navy, Army and Air Force Institutes, created by the British Government in 1921, which ran 7,000 canteens during World War Two.

Tuesday, 8th May

Still at Borghorst, we were informed early this morning that there would definitely be no air transport for this camp today, so we were at last able to plan out our day without fear of recall. I took a leisurely breakfast at 9am, after which I walked up into town and went to see the second talkie picture of my free life; I don't think I'd gone to a movie before noon before in my life.

After dinner I got a haircut from one of the German hairdressers who come into camp for that purpose. No holiday for them, you will notice. Have felt shockingly tired and lethargic all day, and with a bit of tummy trouble again. Food up at the messes now too much for me instead of not enough. Had a little nap after the haircut but got rushed off to Croydon Hall by a report that all RAF were wanted there and would be getting transport out to the 'drome. Of course nothing came of it, and cost us all a lot of trouble for nothing.

Upon finally hearing that we will not be drawing out tonight, I returned to my billet and bed, and had another nap. It is now 8.45pm, so I shall find a place by a radio somewhere to hear the King speak at 9pm. I was too exhausted to lift myself from my bed to hear the Premier at 3pm this afternoon.

Wednesday, 9th May

09.30

Informed moving out to airstrip 10.00 for transit to England.

Rheine RAF Station, Germany[31]

13.00

Left Borghorst 11am. Arrived Rheine RAF station 12 noon. Very large airfield, much bombed by both Allies and Jerries in their turn. The scene is rather like a tip for aged aircrafts. Bags of Lancs around and shifting off pretty fast but also bags of bods awaiting airlift. Shouldn't think we'll get off today, as only two runways left serviceable.

Town of Rheine very much in ruins. Lovely hot day. Given tents to stay in. Water situation pretty bad. Don't know just what the score is re grub. Brought scant rations of beef and biscuits with us. NAAFI is going to give us a cake in about an hour.

Machines taking off very fast just now. Almost every three mins. Lying outside of tent in shirtsleeves and not worrying much. Lots of RAF trying to get priority and thus disorganising what organisation there might be here. Have heard we'll be here for perhaps three days. Alright if weather stays like this – though I'd much prefer England.

Think myself there should be some priority for old POWs (like self, of course). At last camp slept above chappie captured in Rhine crossing (towing gliders) six weeks ago. He gets home same time as I do. Ah well.

---

31   Rheine is a town in the district of Steinfurt in Westphalia, north-western Germany.

19.30

Have got to stay the night here, since one of our transports crashed on taking off and burned furiously on the runway for the best of the afternoon, thus holding up operations. Should get off first thing tomorrow morning, weather permitting and machines being available. Have been transferred from army care into hands of RAF more or less officially now, and boy, do the RAF chuck out the grub. More steak, peas and potatoes and bread and jam and tea than ever.

Quite strange to be living on a 'drome again, this time among Dakotas, Mossies, Lancs, Stirlings and other machines that until today I'd barely seen, and certainly not from on the deck. 4,000lb bombs too, kicking around in odd places. Been quite a battle going on all day between RAF transport organisers and army transport organisers. It seems the army's transport is by means of Dakotas, which don't turn up, so they home in on the Lancs, which are organised by our own squadrons back home especially for us RAF chaps – which makes our turn about three times as slow coming round. Still, tomorrow will suit me, as long as there are not too many tomorrows.

Thursday, 10th May
17.20
All aboard the jolly old Lancs at 1600hrs and now writing sitting in a very uncomfortable position somewhere deep down in the bowels of the aircraft, from where I can see absolutely nothing save the rows of nitrogen bottles straight ahead of me. It has been a day of waiting but with much eating too; the food

the RAF served out to us on that 'drome was really good. Some evidence of this fact can be obtained from my pack, which I had stored behind the communicating door here – a poor chappie just had the misfortune to vomit on it! Perhaps the misfortune is more mine than his, but anyway I have discarded the bag (a very neat little ruckpack which I made myself) and tied up the two Red Cross boxes it contained into one package, so no harm done.

17.28

Well, we have been on our way through the air now for one and a quarter hours and are due to cross the English coast at Bradwell Bay, just north of the Thames Estuary, at 17.40, in 12 mins time, so as I write we are still over the North Sea. It is a pity I cannot see out of the aircraft to view the shores of dear old Blighty roll into sight and then for the delightful English countryside to unroll beneath my eyes but I must content myself with knowing that I am over it, or will soon be, and soon after that, shall be—

I have just seen it. A little square of window somebody has uncovered to give us just a glimpse. It's just a smudge so far and there's quite a lot of water between it and us but I've seen it and we cross it in – four and three-quarter mins.

It's coming up and taking shape. This ship's awfully crowded but there's just a little slit I can look through between two other chappies' legs.

17.52
The green fields of England, I have seen them again after four and three-quarter years, the longest years of my life. I believe another half-hour's flying will see us at our destination (near Guildford, I understand) and I shall step out onto my native soil with a single prayer of thankfulness in my heart: to God who has preserved me; to the many boys who have died for me; and for those whom I love, and who love me.

17.53
Over London now.
ETA Dunsfold: 18.04.

18.04
Going into land now.

18.14
Landed. Dunsfold, England.

21.15
Now writing aboard our plane, before Southern Railway special takes us to Cosford [Shropshire]. Since that last entry chronicling my landing in this country, I have experienced the most warm and amazing reception that any of us could possibly have imagined.

The aircraft pulled over to the tarmac, from where we walked towards the buildings. We could not reach them before being clasped warmly by the hand by various uniformed ladies and gentlemen, who were all smiles and said how glad they were to see us home again. Before I knew where I was, I was flat upon my back, having de-lousing powder puffed up my trouserlegs and sleeves – with appreciable force. Then there was a shout of 'Right!' and I got up dazedly as someone said, 'Let me carry your kit'. I passed along between a lot more uniformed ladies and RAF officers who continued to smile, shake my hand, smile, give me cigs, etc., all the while guiding me towards the hangar.

In the hangar was a most glorious layout of flags, bunting, flowers and food. The people there – the RAF staff, WAAF, Red Cross and WVS volunteers[32] – all were just too good to us and couldn't do enough for us.

'Have some tea.'

'Have a sandwich, cake, cigarette.'

They were, I think, rather surprised that we didn't eat more, but the RAF over at Rheine could probably explain that to them. Moreover, some of these dear ladies would be surprised if they knew how much food was surreptitiously consumed – once she had passed on – by an ex-POW who had just politely refused it.

At the tables I had a very nice little chat with an extremely charming and sympathetic little WAAF, the first English girl I had talked with for almost five years. Later, in a beautiful armchair, RAF personnel still insisted on bringing us cakes and tea and things, and I had long chats with those who gave me the 'griff' on England today.

---

32   WVS is the Women's Voluntary Services.

At 22.30, we left by lorry for Cranleigh [Surrey] railway station, and there we found quite a little crowd to welcome us and cheer us as we left at 23.00. Lots of room on the train and rations of lettuce sandwiches, biscuits and cake given us.

Thus we are all exceedingly pleased and grateful for a really grand reception back into this country. And all I can add at the moment is that I am exceedingly happy and tired, and that we are all due to draw into Cosford at 03.55 tomorrow.

RAF Station, Cosford, Shropshire
Friday, 11th May
06.45

I am afraid our train didn't do so well. It was 04.30 before we arrived here, since which time I have done a little documentation, sent telegram home, had hot breakfast of liver, peas and potatoes, with coffee, prunes and sweet, filled in a couple more forms, had cold shower, allotted rooms, very nice rooms, and am at last in bed. Exceedingly nice bed, beautiful white sheets and a pyjama suit, all clean and smelling lovely and fresh and sweet. Yes, it's good to be alive. We are free now until 4pm, and I figure I'm going to fill in a lot of the time asleep.

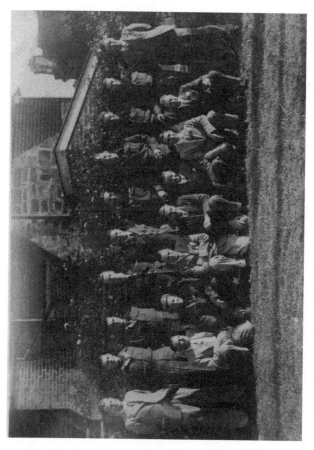

Ex-prisoners of war assembled on their return to Mayfield, East Sussex.
Richard is furthest left in the front row.

POSTSCRIPT BY THE AUTHOR'S GRANDSON

Richard Wicker, my mother's father, died on 22nd November 1980, one year and five months before I was born. When two years ago Mum first handed me that dog-eared brown envelope containing 'Dad's book', I accepted it with mixed feelings. Though intrigued, I couldn't help but think to myself, 'the last thing any of us needs right now is another war story'.

As Britain seeks to break ties with Europe and populist politicians stoke resentment and fear of immigrants, we commemorate the world wars ever more vociferously. Nostalgic for old certainties, 'the war' is depicted as our defining national triumph: valiant underdogs wresting victory from the jaws of defeat once again; *remembrance lest we remember*. But as I leafed through the furled, musty-scented pages of 'Dad's book' I found none of this myth-making. Instead I discovered something different, and infinitely more powerful: a man torn from his life. My grandfather.

The war for Richard is neither glorious nor heroic; it is incarceration, a long and terrible suspension of freedom – not merely a hiatus but a brutal rupture that changes his life for ever. War, in this sense, is pure privation, the opposite to life: abhorrent and unwritable. It's no accident, therefore, that Richard's narrative ends as his war is about to begin, at Waddington Aerodrome on the evening of Wednesday, 28th August 1940: *After tonight, tomorrow, Friday, I was leaving for a long weekend… Just one more flight.*

The weekend never comes; on that last flight, a bombing raid over Cologne, his Hampden plane is shot down. Pilot Cedric Dunkels is killed, while Richard and the two other crew – co-pilot T. G. Hynes and Sergeant L. H. Wainwright – bail out and parachute to earth, where they are taken prisoner. In a letter to his mother less than three weeks later, Richard is jokily upbeat: 'We are firmly convinced we will be home by this Xmas, so you might just tell Churchill to finish it up by 3rd Dec so as to give us a chance to get some nuts.' He would miss this and four more Christmases.

For Richard, as for many millions of others, war is a scar in time. Four years and eight months, from age twenty-seven to thirty-two – what should have been the prime of his life – irretrievably lost. He tries to write his way back, to reimagine a life not yet warped and haunted by loss. In the opening scene, he is standing on a street corner in an unnamed town in northern Germany, unshaven and unfree. He sees himself fading away; people pass by oblivious *that beneath this old man exterior there stood a young man with a young man's desires, thoughts, hopes.* Torn from the familiar, deprived of all the essential *little things in life* – solitude, sunsets, strolls along country lanes – he is unrecognisable if not invisible: a young man turning into a ghost.

Richard never spoke to his family about his experience of war, and we can only estimate its effects on him. He arrived back in Britain emaciated, weighing just seven and a half stone. Although he spares us the grimmest details, we know that life for POWs grew steadily harsher as the war dragged on. Richard and his fellow prisoners were literally starving as they were marched across northern Germany in spring 1945. On 19th April, just as the platoon reached a Red Cross outpost and began unwrapping their food parcels, they were strafed by RAF Typhoons.

This is the account of Bill Garrioch, another POW involved that day, as told by Victor Gammon:[33]

When the attack ended, Garrioch scrambled to his feet, relieved to find himself unhurt. Then he saw what had happened to the Canadian who had been walking beside him. The man's legs and lower torso lay in the road beside Garrioch, the upper half of his body was in the branches of a nearby tree. His face looked quite normal.

Thirty-five men had been killed, many more seriously injured.

Many of the survivors were so shocked and dazed, writes Gammon, *that they could only ask who had survived, so many of the dead were unrecognisable. Tears of deep sorrow and frustration*

---

33 Gammon, V. F. (1996). *Not All Glory,* Weidenfeld Military.

overcame men hardened to death and war. These were their close friends, they had endured years of captivity and its hardships together. Now, with freedom and a reunion with their loved ones perhaps only days away, they were dead, killed by men of their service.

The value of friendship among POWs is difficult for us to fully grasp, being so different from our own often tenuous attachments in twenty-first-century peacetime. Writing in his logbook at the end of the war, Richard paid tribute to fellow POW Paddy Taylor.

An Ode to a Friend
(For J. 'Paddy' Taylor)

I am glad to know him:
He has been to me a staunchly loyal friend through four years' adversity.
He is not the type that smiles, gushes, shakes your hand
And then rushes quickly from you when your plight demands
A service that will mean a little self-denial.

He stands unobtrusively close by your side,
And when you need it, will give you half of what he has,
And having given, waits not for thanks, repayment, retribution.
Rather, his aim all through life – a life of quiet service – and his joy:
Do unto others as you would have them do to you.

After the war, Richard could not bring himself to reveal the full psychological impact of his experiences. He met and began dating seventeen-year-old Winifred Pettitt –

his future wife, my grandmother – shortly after returning home to Mayfield in summer 1945. (His relationship with Connie Lodge petered out.) In a letter to Winifred dated 5th August 1945, he wrote:

'Your assurance that you do enjoy our little trips is very comforting, Wynn, but I know that I'm a very dull companion and a poor hand at general conversation, which my years stuck in isolated prison camps in Germany have done nothing to improve. So great was my sorrow and so utter was the demoralising effect the life had upon me that I once did not speak a single word for three months.' With Winifred, his silences go unnoted. 'That's what I like about you. I can fall silent for quite long periods and the silence between us does not seem to be embarrassing.'

The war may have rendered him taciturn, but it also enhanced his self-confidence and underpinned his conviction that all men are equal – regardless of class or social status. This life lesson, outlined in a letter to Winifred dated 3rd January 1946, warrants quoting in full:

'When I first joined the RAF, I was lodging with a toffee-nosed crowd of blokes. They were all public school boys just out of Cambridge, Oxford, Eton and Harrow and all the high-class schools. In this time, they were always talking about high social positions and their dad's Buick or Rolls and their yachts and their big house in Berkeley Square and how their father was managing director of this and that firm, etc.

In the classroom, they would giggle very superiorly if one of the lower-class boys couldn't answer a question in trigonometry or algebra, just because we hadn't had such a good education. When they questioned me about my private life, you may well imagine that it was pretty embarrassing for me to say that I was educated at an elementary school and that I had to start work when I was 12 because my people were very poor and my dad was only a chimney sweep.

Well, when we finished with classroom and started in practical application, I found that as far as gumption or common sense were concerned, they hadn't the slightest idea of how to take things to pieces and put them together again. They were hopeless, and I streaked miles ahead of them. In German prison camps, when it came to looking out for themselves, washing their own clothes, darning their own socks and keeping themselves clean, they were like a lot of helpless babies. That taught me a lesson, and now whoever I meet and have to interview or talk with, I can always look them straight in the eye and think to myself: I may not be better, but at least I'm as good as everybody I meet.'

Immersing myself in the words of the grandfather I never knew has been profoundly and mysteriously rewarding. I *recognise* Richard as I read him, almost hearing his voice as I imagine the bond that could have been. His quietly determined temperament, meritocratic instinct and writing ambition are traits I'd like to believe I share with him. Whether or not that's wishful thinking, he has renewed in me a faith in writing independent of the vagaries of publication and praise. By bearing witness and recording his experience, Richard left behind a trace, a taste, a guide-rope across time – what a precious gift.

This is a book not about war and destruction but about what remains intact and must be cherished: love, freedom, and the cumulatively inestimable 'small things in life'. In short, Richard came home knowing what mattered to him – the same things that matter to us all, if only we could pause to take stock. In a letter to Winifred on 2nd February 1946, he daydreams their future together:

'In the summer you could come down to Glynde by train and I could meet you and we could go for lovely walks up on the Lewes Downs, and walk until we got tired, and then lie and bask in the hot sunshine and look out over the sea and think how good it was to be alive and how lucky we were to have such a beautiful friendship as ours.

Don't you think that would be lovely, Wynn? We could even take some grub and a flask of tea and stay on the hill and picnic beside a dew-pond, and afterwards I could lie with my head in your lap and you could read *Romeo and Juliet* or *My Son, My Son* to me until I fell asleep and then you could put the book down and go to sleep too and we would wake up when it was quite dark and your hair would be covered with dew and your eyes would be very sleepy and you'd look very lovely. We'd walk back down the hill arm in arm under the stars and everything would be quiet and peaceful and still, and we'd both be very happy.'

David Bradford, February 2019

Richard and Winifred on holiday in
Margate, Kent, 15th June 1948.